Making memories that last

The Principle Trust Children's Charity

The story of the first 10 years

FISHER KING PUBLISHING

Fisher King Publishing
The Old Barn
York Road
Thirsk
YO7 3AD
England
www.fisherkingpublishing.co.uk

This book is dedicated to my mum, Lilia Emily Davies, who died aged 45 on 26th July 1956 when I was five years old.

For any child to have to grow up without the love of their mother is something I would not want to happen to anyone.

Charity Founder Mike Davies MBE

Yorkshire Rose

Foreword From
Captain Sir Thomas Moore

I am delighted and honoured that we have been asked to write the Foreword for this fabulous book, which looks back over the first nine years of The Principle Trust Children's Charity.

We also look forward to hearing more about the Charity's successes in the future and how it has continued to support and help children, families, and carers in its 10th year.

It is wonderful how this special charity and its team provide much needed time and space for underprivileged, disadvantaged, and disabled children by granting them free holidays.

My father, Captain Sir Tom, is a Yorkshireman and was delighted to learn that the charity is based close to Keighley, where he was born and had a fabulously adventurous time when he was growing up.

The charity helps children, many of whom have never a break in their lives, by giving them the precious gift of time to enjoy themselves in a relaxing environment. Whether it is at the seaside, the stunning countryside of Ribble Valley, or picturesque shores of Lake Windermere.

It is holiday memories that children treasure forever. Hours spent splashing at the water's edge, discovering exciting nature trails, and eating together, with friends or family, are magical and important moments, however simple they may seem.

My sister and I had many glorious times away with my mother and father. Everything was exciting about the trips: from counting down the days until the holidays began, seeing packed suitcases in the

hall and the car journey leading us to our destination for days of fun. We adored being together, exploring, discovering, chatting, and laughing. It undoubtedly made our family closer and stronger and I know how lucky we were.

Whatever your age, being able to recharge batteries, and totally relax, is vital to everyone's health and wellbeing. Without exception, every child deserves time off in a safe, peaceful, and loving environment to have the freedom to think, create, and be themselves.

Hannah Ingram-Moore (Tom's daughter) and Captain Sir Tom

The Principle Trust Children's Charity has done a phenomenal job, over that ten years, in giving over 3,600 children a free holiday. Many of them come from loving families who, for a number of reasons, are struggling financially, or they have had traumatic experiences that have led them to live in foster or care

homes and just need some time away. During the Pandemic, the charity has also organised holidays for several Key Workers and people on the Front Line which has allowed them to spend an enjoyable period with their families.

Long may The Principle Trust Children's Charity continue to provide hope, kindness, and love to hundreds of deserving children, for decades to come.

Keep up the good work.

Hannah Ingram-Moore - 2020.

Mike Davies MBE, Captain Sir Tom, and Brenda Davies
at 'An Evening with Captain Sir Tom' at The Coniston Hotel, 2020.

Tribute To Captain Sir Tom Moore
1920 – 2021

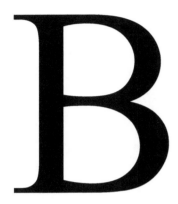

renda and I were delighted to be asked by Michael and Nick Bannister of The Coniston Hotel to attend 'An Evening with Captain Sir Tom Moore and his family'. The opportunity to meet the great man and his family was a chance of a lifetime.

What a charming man he was! Captain Sir Tom was only too pleased to allow us to have a photograph taken with him, which we will treasure.

Captain Sir Tom was very interested in The Principle Trust Children's Charity and the work we undertake.

He told us of his early life in Keighley, and how he used to like to go to Skipton for a day out, particularly on Market Day and how he enjoyed seeing all the animals there.

I asked Captain Sir Tom and Hannah his daughter if they would be kind enough to write a few words by way of an introduction to the book. They were delighted to have been asked and their foreword/introduction is included, along with a lovely photograph of Captain Sir Tom with Hannah.

Brenda and I were incredibly sad when we learned about Captain Sir Tom passing away after having contracted Covid-19.

Our sincere condolences go to all Captain Sir Tom's family. His legacy will live on for many generations to come. What he achieved for the NHS was simply incredible. We are delighted that The Captain Tom Foundation has been established which is a fitting memory to an incredible man.

WINDSOR CASTLE

19ᵗʰ October 2020

Dear Mr. Davies,

The Queen wishes me to write and thank you for your letter in which you tell her about your charity's continuing work for underprivileged, disadvantaged and disabled children in Yorkshire.

Her Majesty was very glad to hear that the Principle Trust Children's Charity has also been offering free holidays to key workers and their families, in some of your holiday homes during this Covid-19 year.

In your letter you tell The Queen that, as next year is the 10ᵗʰ Anniversary of the Principle Trust Children's Charity, one of your supporters has offered to publish a book about the splendid work you do. Although Her Majesty is unable to write a foreword to the book as you ask, she would be very glad to see a copy of it when it is finished.

I am to thank you again for writing to The Queen and I do hope that the new book will be able to spread the word, as you suggest, about the excellent aims of your charity.

Yours sincerely,

Susan Hussey.

Lady-in-Waiting

Mr M Davies MBE

2020-0063936VFPO

Vicky Ford MP
Parliamentary Under-Secretary of State for Children and Families

Sanctuary Buildings 20 Great Smith Street Westminster London SW1P 3BT
tel: 0370 000 2288 www.education.gov.uk/help/contactus

Mike Davies MBE
The Principle Trust Children's Charity
By email: info@theprincipletrust.co.uk

23 November 2020

Dear Mike,

Thank you for your letter of 5 October, addressed to the Prime Minister, outlining the work of The Principle Trust Children's Charity. Your letter has been passed to this department and I am replying as the minister responsible for this policy area. I apologise for the delay in responding.

May I begin by wishing you well in these challenging times. I am very grateful to the Principle Trust Children's Charity for the wonderful work that they do. We know how valuable short breaks and respite are for families raising children and young people with additional needs – not only allowing young people themselves to develop skills, wider social networks and independence, but also giving their parents a much-needed rest from caring responsibilities.

Congratulations on the upcoming 10th Anniversary of the charity and the publication of your book, which I am sure will provide an important resource for families and organisations that work with them. I am happy to provide a quote for the foreword, as follows:

'My congratulations and thanks to The Principle Trust Children's Charity for the publication of this book, which is a testament to their important work with disadvantaged families. Holidays and respite care can be invaluable for those families who would not otherwise be able to enjoy spending quality family time together away from the stresses at home.'

I wish you continued success with the work of the charity and the very best of luck with the new book.

Yours sincerely,

Vicky Ford.

Vicky Ford MP
Parliamentary Under-Secretary of State for Children and Families

Mike's Dad (David), Mum (Lillia), and Mike

Charity Founder Mike Davies MBE Shares His Story

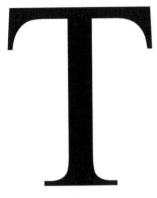he records on my birth certificate state I arrived on 5th January 1951, at York Road Maternity Hospital, Battersea, London. Mum, Lillia Emily Davies, and Dad, David Owen Davies a Milk Roundsman.

What the certificate does not show, but I have been informed of, was that I weighed in at 11lbs. A whopper, which must have been a weight for my mum to carry around for the last few months of her pregnancy.

I have also been informed that in the next bed in the maternity ward was a mum with a baby daughter, also born on the 5th who weighed in at 5lbs 7oz. Virtually half my weight. The nurses referred to us as Sampson and Delilah. No need to guess which one I was! Whilst not born within earshot of the sound of the Bow Bells I have been referred to as a Cockney many a time.

I became the youngest of four siblings and evened up the numbers to two of each sex. Jean, my eldest sister was 17 years old when I was born, David was 12 years old, and Joan was 7 years old.

What I was unaware of at this stage was that on 26th July 1956, some five years and six months later my Mum, Lillia Emily Davies, would be taken from us, and tragically die from cancer. Mum was 45 years old when she died and suffered badly fighting the disease for a number of years. Mum was buried on 31st July 1956, at Morden Cemetery in a family plot, meaning there would be room for Dad when he passed away.

At the time when Mum died, Jean had married and moved with her husband to Liverpool. David was about to leave home and undertake National Service in the army, which left Dad, Joan at 12 years old, and me at 5 years old at home.

Neither Joan nor I went to the funeral. One of our cousins took us out for the day to London Zoo. So, at the time of Mum's burial, we were having fun at the Zoo. I guess that was the right thing to do to keep us occupied.

I never really was informed or sat down and had it explained to me that Mum had died. I was used to her not being at home and being in hospital "because she was ill", and even when she was at home a great deal of her time was spent in bed feeling unwell. I assume that I just got used to Mum not being there and did not question too much or understand that she was not coming home.

I can vaguely recall one holiday with Mum and Dad, when we went to visit Mum's brother and sister-in-law, Uncle Bill, and Aunty Ive. Uncle Bill was a Factory Manager for Tate and Lyle Sugar Refiners and had a lovely house in the countryside very near to the factory. They were unable to have children for whatever reason thus made a fuss of me, which was great! They had a German Shepherd dog called Pooch, who I got on famously with. He used to sleep on the end of my bed, which I loved. Pooch would come out with me and Uncle Bill into the fields early in the mornings when we picked mushrooms, and Pooch chased the rabbits and birds. I used to love Uncle Bill and Aunty Ive. She was a real Cockney and would have given Del Trotter a run for his money with her rhyming slang! My eldest sister Jean told me in later life that Uncle Bill and Aunty Ive approached my Dad and asked if they could adopt me. Dad said no, which I was obviously unaware of. I cannot recall any other holiday with Mum and Dad.

I have during my life wondered what it would have been like growing up with a Mum, but there is no answer as I will never know. I could see the other more fortunate kids with their Mums and Dads sharing good times together, holidays, trips out, treats, a car and a tv! Was I envious? I guess I was, but my eldest sister Jean (from afar) and sister Joan tried to do Mum things for me and with me.

So, life got very different and extremely tough. Jean and David had left home. Dad, whom was out at work delivering milk for The London Coop from 5am each morning, Joan at 12 years old and me at 5 years old. Joan and I got very close and she looked after me as much as she could. She would get me ready for primary school, make breakfast for us, and then I walked to school with some other children whilst Joan went to secondary school in another direction.

Other kids had Mums and Dads taking them and collecting them from school. Sometimes my Dad would collect me. I wished my Mum would be there for me.

Home life was difficult for the three of us. I think I can recall a holiday which Dad, Joan, and I went to Ramsgate on the South Coast. We went by train from Clapham Junction. Only an hour and a half away. I recall the beach, the amusements, and having a bag of chips on the way back to the bed and breakfast we stayed in.

Money was very tight, and there was not much to spare on things like a telephone, a car, colour tv, or spending money for treats or sweets, or cinema etc…

Dave came home from the army to visit and Jean came from Liverpool occasionally to see us. I looked forward to Jean and her husband David coming to visit. They brought me treats and spoiled me. I just wished they lived nearer so I could get to visit them more easily.

I do recall Dad arranging with the council for us to have a "Home Help", a lady employed by the council who would come to our flat to clean, launder, and cook a meal. This was very necessary as Dad could not manage to do everything and work as well. I assume it was no real surprise that Dad got very close to the Home Help who was a divorcee herself with two daughters. Thus, within a few years Dad and Betty (the Home Help) married, Betty and her two daughters then moved into our tiny flat. Dad arranged with the council for us to move to a bigger council house some 4 miles away, which meant I had to change school and lose all the friends I had made. I was very unhappy for a long time, even though the new primary school was only 100 yards from our new home.

Life got even tougher for me. I became the only boy with 3 girls in our house. I never really got on with my stepsisters. Money got tighter as Dad had more mouths to feed, clothe, and look after.

I resented the other family's intrusion and I recognise that I went off the rails somewhat. Schoolwork suffered and I would get into trouble for misbehaving. I admit to stealing sweets, helping myself to some small amounts of money, and got in with some other boys who were likeminded (but did have mums). I would do anything to get out of schoolwork and did not enjoy homelife. I had no real "new clothes". Dad used to get clothes from second-hand shops (whether they fitted me or not!). This affected me and my mates would "take the Mickey" about my second-hand clothes and attire.

Dad and Betty went on to have two children together. Both girls, June, and Susan. The house got even busier, less time for the only boy in the house, money was tighter than ever before. I liked life even less and yearned for the day I could leave and get away.

Yes, we had some holidays, back to Ramsgate on the train. I honestly cannot recall the holidays being memorable.

I got a newspaper delivery round at 11 years old which earned me £1 per week (equivalent to circa £22 per week today!) which was great. Dad took half of the money, so I did not squander it! It helped me save towards train fares and holidays to Liverpool to spend time with Jean and David. At last, I had some money, not a lot but some to spend.

I can vividly recall arranging to go to Liverpool to stay with Jean and David on the train from Euston to Liverpool Lime Street for the summer holidays. Six weeks away! Dad took me on the bus to Euston. He found me a seat on the train and asked the person sat next to me if he or she would keep an eye on me until I got to Liverpool. In those days, the train journey was about six hours, so I was sat next to strangers, them looking after me. I did this from about 11 years old onwards. I can recall having a carrier bag with my clothes in! Usually, the strangers took pity on me and treated me to sweets, crisps, and drinks during the journey, and a few of them even gave me some money to spend in Liverpool, great! I simply could not envisage doing this today and asking someone to look after my son for a six-hour train journey.

Trips to Liverpool were fantastic. I loved them. My own bedroom, a car, colour tv, trips out, and some new clothes (that fit!). Jean and David's friends used to make a fuss of me and welcomed me to their homes. This was more of the life I enjoyed.

Often during the summer holidays, we would travel to Scotland where David came from and stay with his family there. We would go fishing in the Glens, go to the seaside, go camping, walking, and really have a good time. I quickly began to feel that I wanted to spend more time in Liverpool, and less in the life I had in London.

However, I had to conclude secondary schooling. Unbelievably I won a scholarship to Emanuel School, largely due to my brother David going to the school, so I won a Governor's place at the school. I cannot to this day understand how I got accepted.

The uniform had to be purchased from Harrods! Nowhere else. It must have cost Dad (and my 50% paper round money) a week's salary for that first uniform. It was the only one which came from Harrods. From then on, I would buy from the school shop and wear second-hand clothes.

I needed to get from 11 to 17 years old before considering what to do after schooling. Emanuel was, and still is a very prestigious school, excelling academically, with many famous, clever people having studied there. Sporting achievements in rowing, rugby, cricket, and athletics to name a few are very strongly developed, with many famous sportsmen (and now women) having been educated at Emanuel.

I was in the lowest set, along with circa 12 other boys, and we studied through from 11 years old to 16 years old when 0 Levels were sat. Studied is probably an overused word here! Yes, we attended school. No, we were not the brightest sparks, but we were all mates.

I cannot say I enjoyed school. Far too disciplined for me. Yes, I got the "stick" a few times, and yes it hurt. On the backside or on the hand. I could never get my head around Latin, never had an interest in English literature, divinity (RE) was a waste to me as I could never believe that a God would take my Mum from me at just 5 years old. Physics was boring and the music I liked was not the music which Christian Strover our Music Teacher taught.

Mike's Dad (David) and Mike
with Pooch the dog

Economic history got too involved and as for trigonometry… well let's not talk about that. I guess a lack of application, understanding, and very limited revision had to have the outcome it had. Likewise, I continued to have an awkward home life, not wanting to be at home, spend time elsewhere, and wanting to be away from London. Thus the 0 Level results brought nil gains, and the stark reality at 16 years and 7 months old of what to do now?!

This was the watershed time in my life, and I realised it. A very unhappy childhood, no Mum to turn to. Not wanting to be in London. No qualifications, I could not continue studying having flopped all my exams. Little chance of a career. What happens now?!

I had to speak with my brother-in-law David and my brother David. Both were very successful in commerce careers. I proposed a potential approach to the police as they had cadets which were training grounds for the police as a career. You could apply for entry at 17 years old until 19 years old then progress into the regular force. I approached the Liverpool and Bootle Police Cadets, sat the exams, had the interviews, the physical and medical exams, and was accepted as a police cadet from 8th January 1968. Yes, success!

Before I left London there was one thing I had to do. I wanted to go and visit Mum's grave and pay my respects and tell her what I was about to do. To let her know that I was not leaving her and that I would be back to visit and let her know how I was getting on. Dad gave me the grave details. But he told me there was not a headstone, only a plot number. Having arrived at Morden Cemetery, I enquired at the office where the general direction was, and I was given the details. I found the line of plots. A few had headstones most did not, just grass and weeds over a piece of ground with some small numbers on a metal sign in the ground. I could not accurately find Mum's numbered plot 2215 in FL area. I hunted and paced some measures from one which was numbered, but I could not accurately find my Mum's grave. I was devastated. Where was my Mum? Why had there never been a headstone put on her grave? I had to give up looking. I cried and cried. This was the first time I had asked to come and see Mum's grave and I could not be sure where it was. I was distraught. How could this be? I swore to myself then, that I would try and get a headstone put at the correct spot where Mum was buried so I could come and pay respects when I could. I left not having that discussion with Mum but knowing in my heart that I would be back.

I left London on 1st January 1968, with Jean and David in their car. My worldly possessions and clothes in bags heading for Liverpool.

I had left behind the unhappy childhood, the real difficulties of losing Mum. The difficulties of Joan and I looking after each other at 12 and 5 years old. The second-hand clothes, missing out on so many childhood activities and without a qualification to my name!

I had often said to myself that I never wanted any child of mine to grow up in similar circumstances to me. I wanted good things for any family I would have. I would work hard and hopefully earn money to give my family things that I never had. I hoped that cancer would never play a part in my family life as it had done with Mum and her children. I want new clothes, treats for my family, fun holidays to put smiles on faces, and create happy memories. I had hoped that I could provide this for my family and keep them away from any underprivileged or disadvantaged situations. I did not want my family to grow up like I did.

The 6th January 1968, the day after my 17th birthday, I reported to The Police Training School in Mather Avenue Liverpool, less than 2 miles from where my sister and brother-in-law lived, and just one mile away from Penny Lane and Strawberry Fields, which were the locations which The Beatles sang about.

On reflection, the decision to select and try to join the police cadets was a brilliant masterstroke of strategic thinking and careful considerations on my behalf.

I wish that were the case and it was true!

It was actually a simple process of deduction which I hoped would give me the opportunity of going back to further education, to college to study whilst in the cadets, whilst giving me the opportunity of gaining an insight into the police force as a career, and one major benefit being I would get paid a wage for being a cadet! An easy decision given my upbringing, difficult home life, poor levels of study in schools, and making choices which were clearly wrong along the way.

From the minute I walked through the training school door, and for the next two years of being a cadet, my life changed for the better!

The navy-blue uniform had you looking like a Police Constable. The difference being you had no powers of arrest, a flat hat with a blue band around it, and of course the short back and sides haircut!

Being cadet #91 was the makings of me and helped me develop, grow up, and mature in a host of ways.

Year 1 had cadets working 5.5 days per week. 4 days studying at Childwall College, then 1.5 days (including Saturday mornings) at Police Training School learning a little more about police work. In college you wore "civilian clothes" but were instantly recognisable from the haircut! At Training College, you wore uniform, and learned to respect senior officers with military like respect, saluting, standing to attention, speaking when spoken to etc… But you were encouraged to develop as a person in many ways.

You lived in at the Training School for 3 months and learned cooking, cleaning, washing, ironing, and many household chores which hitherto were alien to me! You were encouraged to be involved in sporting activities, and if you showed signs of aptitude in any sport, you were elevated to selection for the force team, which was an honour! Fortunately, I was a good swimmer, rugby player, and cricketer. I was chosen to represent the force at lifesaving competitions and travelled the country as a member of the Liverpool and Bootle Police Life Saving Team in competitions. I was The Cricketer of the Year in 1969 and still have the wooden trophy suitably engraved. I managed a few games for the force rugby team but there were bigger, fitter, more hardy brutes than me in the team. Of course, if you were in the sporting teams, you received exemption from many other activities which suited me fine!

I managed to achieve many awards for swimming and lifesaving. This was a key issue in the force as every member of the force had to be able to swim as we were a port force with The River Mersey, and The Irish Sea touching several parts of the force boundaries. The highlight was being presented the Distinction Award by the Chief Constable and getting my photo in the local press. Wow, what a turnaround. Me with the Chief Constable for doing something really good, very different from my earlier days in Battersea sailing close to the law for my antics!

Without doubt one of the biggest changes in me was due to The Duke of Edinburgh's Awards Scheme which all cadets had to undertake. Apart from the outward-bound activities, the orienteering, camping expeditions in the mountains in North Wales, the elements I really looked forward to was the "volunteering periods" (which were not volunteering by the cadets – you had to undertake them!). For the Bronze Award I went to a Home for Forgotten Allies near Doncaster in Yorkshire. Along with about 8 other volunteers from different walks of life we were provided with paint, brushes, and lots of rooms to decorate in a very large old building which housed forgotten foreign people from World War II. We lived outside under canvas for two weeks and spent each day painting and decorating the building and bedrooms. Many of the people living there could not speak English, and my Hungarian and Russian was not too good. Learning to communicate via sign language was fun. A learning experience which was all new to me!

For the Silver DofE Award I was seconded to The YMCA in Nottingham. I was one of two cadets, the other being a guy from Southampton force called John. It was great fun and only a few hundred yards from The YWCA. We did all the chores and tasks which the manager, a guy named Ray Collins asked of us. John and I had a competition going when we were on the front reception desk. When we needed to speak on the announcer requesting someone to contact us, we used to pronounce their name backwards! So, we would go onto the loudspeaker asking Mr Yar Snilloc (Ray Collins) to contact reception. Obviously, no one contacted us. Ray soon sussed us out and saw the funny side of things! We had a great 3 months there. I recall decorating the sports hall, which took ages, and multitudes of paint cans, whilst listening over and over to The Beatles

Abbey Road album. I reckon I learned every word of every song (and still know many of the words now!).

The Gold Award for DofE Scheme had me volunteering at a Leonard Cheshire Home in Littleborough near Rochdale. This experience changed my life and my approach to people much less fortunate than me. Group Captain Leonard Cheshire (husband to Sue Ryder) opened several homes for severely disabled people of all ages. They were not modern today type hospices but did have people living there with life limiting illnesses, and disabilities. I spent three months at the home, working with the matron doing whatever I was asked to do. In many instances I did everything (and I mean everything) for severely disabled people from bathing Jim, whom had to be on a hoist to lift him out of bed, whizz along the ward to the bathroom, then undress him and lower him into the bath. He never complained about anything but gave abuse to the other inmates for them not doing something properly when he could do nothing! Yes, many men required help with ablutions. I drove the ambulance which had been donated by St John's Ambulance Association, taking people to and from hospital appointments. I sat talking to Steven from Liverpool who was bedridden and had a debilitating disease which made him blind. What a laugh we used to have. I would stand outside his bedroom door and try and disguise my voice when speaking to him. He got me every time. I wrote letters from him to his parents and friends. He dictated and I wrote. I would then hold his hand to write his signature at the end of the letter. I was on call 24 hours a day whilst there and had many calls during the night when staff would call me to come and calm down someone who was having nightmares from the war, or forcibly get Ronnie back to bed as he was not going down to the pub at 3am! The men in their ward used to love me reading a short story to them all or reading a few jokes from a joke book. The more risqué the better they liked them. Often one would shout to me "Hey Cockney Mike, tell us a joke, or read us a story!". So little from me, yet so much for them. I never refused!

My time at the Leonard Cheshire Home changed my outlook on life. I was personally helping people to do things which I took so much for granted. People were so grateful to me for helping them. I was offered money and personal items for helping people. I did not accept them of course. But these people were so grateful. In many ways I was reminded of my Mum wanting so much to be here with her family yet being unable to due to cancer. Mum died, at least the people at the home were still alive, but the quality of their lives was not good. I tried to make their lives easier and better in whatever small ways I could.

I knew when my time was up after 3 months that I would miss the home and the folk. I did return about three times over the following 2 years. Some of the guys I knew had very sadly passed away. Then I was informed Steven from Liverpool had died at 26 years old. I cried for him. I went to his funeral in Liverpool. His parents said that he used to talk about me "The Cockney Police Cadet from Liverpool who made him laugh". A reward in itself.

The end of my volunteering stints made me realise that I had something to offer those people less fortunate than myself. I was continually amazed that with such little effort I could make a difference and put a smile on a face. I could make someone happy, help them achieve something, and generally help them cope with their circumstances for however long they had on this earth.

Stored away in the back of my mind was this realisation that "one day in the future, when time and opportunity would allow, I want to do something similar again to help those people less fortunate than myself whomever and wherever they are".

Mike in Police, bottom row, far right

Cadetship was great for me. I studied, sat, and passed 6 x 0 Levels, (which was 6 more than I achieved at school!) although quite what use British Constitution, and general principles of English Law have been to me since I am unsure. I represented the police in many sporting areas, achieved bronze, silver and gold Duke of Edinburgh Awards, met lots of new people, made lots of new friends, had a ridiculously short haircut for two years, lived in Liverpool which I loved, supported the Red Team in Liverpool, and got paid by the police for enjoying life. Seems like a great deal! And a long way from the unhappiness of life after Mum died.

However, even though I was, for the last 6 months of cadetship posted to several different departments throughout the force to try and learn how different departments work, I did not really get a good insight into the role of a Police Officer.

But in January 1970 at 19 years old I became PC 133 F to be stationed at Allerton Road Station in Liverpool. A real PC, with powers of arrest, paid a salary, with a tall hat not a flat one with a blue band around it!

The regular force and a three-shift system of 6am to 2pm, 2pm to 10pm, then 10pm to 6am, this did not fit with me. I could not sleep during the day, could not go out socialising after 10pm, and friends were at work at 2pm. The pay was not great, but there were several perks if you wanted a police house, etc... I did not want the perks at 19 years old! I began to think about a change of career, maybe to follow my brother, brother-in-law into commerce, given that commerce was about dealing and mixing with people, challenges, targets to achieve, initiatives, and regular hours!

In early 1971 I decided to leave the police, and in certain instances with some regrets, but I wanted to progress my career, faster than I would have in the police. Thus, I applied for and was successful in achieving a commerce role with RHM Foods (Ranks Hovis McDougall). Operating in the North West of England, selling a wide range of great consumer brands, and being successful in developing firstly to Training Manager for the North of England, then promoted to an Area Manager responsible for seven men. I was the youngest ever Area Manager at the age of 23 years old. The youngest salesman working for me in the team was twice my age! We were known throughout the company as Dads Army!

I recall one of the salesmen left his raincoat behind at one of our meetings, which I found when tidying everything away, and decided to drop it off at his house in Preston on my way home. I was invited in for a coffee, and there was his youngest daughter Brenda whom I had heard much about. Wow! Apart from being guarded by two ferocious boxer dogs, whom I thought were bull dogs! She was lovely looking, we chatted easily (although I was stood behind an easy chair to keep some space between me and the dogs!) Brenda was a few days away from celebrating her 21st birthday. I asked her (sheepishly) for a date the day after her 21st birthday which she accepted. Phew!

The rest is history!

Brenda and I were married on Remembrance Day 11th November 1976. Regrettably, Brenda's dad passed away suddenly two weeks after we were married. A real shock. He was only 56 years old.

In reality, I did not think it would be acceptable for my father-in-law to work for me thus I had moved from RHM Foods to The Smiths Food Group (Smiths Crisps) in a promoted role in 1975.

Philip our eldest son was born in July 1977.

Smiths was a successful move, but I was offered promotion to HQ in Kew London which I turned down as I did not want, nor could afford to move to London. Having turned down the promotion I thought my days would be numbered thus when I was approached by Cussons UK Ltd (Imperial Leather Soap etc…) in 1980 for another enhanced role based in Manchester, I jumped at the chance.

I was employed by Cussons for 10 years which was a really enjoyable, challenging, and a fun time. I made some really good friends and many of us have an annual reunion in November even now!

Andrew our youngest son was born in 1982, and life for Brenda was bringing up two sons in a better way and more loving environment than the upbringing I had experienced.

I was offered a Directorship with The Robert McBride Personal Care Division in 1990. This role taught me more about strategic management and customer branded business (private label) than anything I had previously learned. Regrettably, I became a victim of the business being sold in 1995 and was made redundant for the first time in my life. An awful feeling, largely due to "why me", "what will I do next", "where will it be" and "what effect will it have on my family?!"

Fortunately, I obtained a Director role for a small health food business based near Bradford. An interesting and growing market not only in the UK but also internationally.

I was appointed Managing Director in 1998, but the parent company an Irish based PLC did not have a desire to grow the branded or private label business. Thus, I left the business in 2000 to start up a consultancy with a business partner which we developed over two years.

Regrettably, my Dad died on 25th January 1996, he died on Brenda's birthday, so it is a date we do not forget for two very different reasons. Dad had a weak heart for a number of years. He was buried with my Mum in the family plot in Morden Cemetery. This was the chance for Dad's offspring to agree collectively to a lovely black marble headstone with Mum and Dad's details inscribed. This gives me the opportunity to visit Mum and Dad's grave and pay my respects to them both. It has gone from being an unmarked grave to one of the nicest in the cemetery!

My brother-in-law David lost his life to cancer in 2001. Without doubt he had been my mentor in business and throughout my career in commerce. He had along with my sister Jean agreed for me to move to Liverpool and live with them whilst developing a career. A huge loss to me, as he would offer help, support, advice, and guidance not only in business but for any issue. He was a very knowledgeable man, we all wanted to be on his team in any family quizzes! Of course, he introduced me to Liverpool Football Club so he will "never walk alone!". I just wish he could be here to have witnessed his help, assistance, and advice come to fruition with the development and growth of the Principle Healthcare Group from 2002 to 2020.

Two years after leaving the health food business, and out of covenant with previous PLC employers, in 2002, I gave up the consultancy to develop a start-up business which was named Principle Healthcare. This was a challenge which I had never experienced before. Our own business from a start-up position, with a vision, a plan, some premises, Barclays Bank behind us, and the world to go for! Yes, we sailed close to the "going bust scenario" but we had a great team of committed people, and 24/7 to make it work! And work it did!

However, a real sad day for me was 17th December 2003 when my sister Joan, died of breast cancer. Poor Joan had lost her husband a year earlier and had fought cancer valiantly for 8 years before she so sadly lost her fight. Thus, my grandma, my mum, and my sister, three generations were to have developed cancer and lost their lives due to it. Joan was 60 years old and left behind three sons. All my early years at home with Joan came back to me. How she looked after me from 5 years old. She was a star and taken too soon. A real sad loss to me.

Principle Healthcare went from strength to strength. Teamwork was the order of the company, and I was fortunate that both my sons worked in the business in different areas.

> In 2006 we developed Principle Healthcare International to grow the business internationally.

> In 2008 we set up a new company and manufacturing facility in Slovakia named Innopharma S.R.O. to develop Central and Western European markets.

> In 2011 we developed and launched The Principle Trust Children's Charity. Providing free holidays for underprivileged and disadvantaged children.

> In 2011 my business partner Richard Doyle and I were invited by The Cabinet Office to attend 10 Downing Street for a meeting with Ministers about apprentices in business. Another experience!

> In 2012 we hit the jackpot with a number of developments. We won The Queen's Award for Enterprise for International Trade resulting in a visit to Buckingham Palace to a reception hosted by Her Majesty, The Queen. I was fortunate enough to be introduced to The Queen and chat about the business. I was on cloud nine! We were presented with The Queen's Award by the Lord Lieutenant for North

Yorkshire, Lord Crathorne visited the business and not only presented us with the award, but also opened our new manufacturing facility named 'Health Innovations'. In addition, we were awarded with the prestigious award of Investors in People Gold Standard which Lord Crathorne presented. He commented that it is unprecedented for him to attend such a company and present three such prestigious awards on the same day.

- In 2014 we launched Principle in Germany. Not the most successful venture largely due to having the wrong team in place! Proving business does not always just progress in an upward direction!

- In 2014 we purchased a small B2C business called Clubvits to capitalise on the growing online trend.

- In 2015 we purchased a company called Vitrition, a contract manufacturing business based in Yorkshire.

- In 2016 we purchased a branded business called Health and Wellbeing Brands to develop our branded portfolio.

On 5th May 2017 I received a letter which had 'On Her Majesty's Service' and 'The Cabinet Office' printed on the outside of the envelope. Another invite to 10 Downing Street? No, much more exciting than that. The letter stated that The Prime Minister is proposing to Her Majesty The Queen that she approve that I be appointed a Member of the Order of the British Empire, an MBE! For services to business and to disadvantaged children in North Yorkshire, attend Buckingham Palace and bring along three guests. That's Brenda, Phil, and Andrew seeing me being appointed with an MBE!

A far cry from that 5-year-old, with no Mum, growing up in a disadvantaged and underprivileged environment, getting into trouble, wearing second-hand clothes, messing about at school, achieving no qualifications, and as my cousin so aptly put it: "Who would have thought that the snotty nosed 5-year-old from Queenstown Road in Battersea, will be at The Palace receiving an MBE?! Unbelievable!".

This has to be the highlight of a varied career and life.

- My family have been and are everything to me.

- My companies, the people, and the enjoyment are incredible.

- The charity developments, the smiles on faces from underprivileged, disadvantaged, and disabled children make everything worthwhile.

Mike receiving his MBE from The Duke of Cambridge - Prince William,
December 2017

Mike Davies and Richard Doyle at 10 Downing Street, attending a
meeting with Ministers about apprentices in business in 2011

Mike Davies talking with Her Majesty The Queen after having received The Queen's Award for Enterprise, International Trade in 2012.

BUCKINGHAM PALACE

5th December, 2012

Dear Mr. Davies and Ms. Lazenby,

The Queen has asked me to thank you for your letter of 26th November, from which Her Majesty was pleased to learn how much you enjoyed your visit to Buckingham Palace, to attend the reception for The Queen's Award for Enterprise winners for 2012.

Your kind words to Her Majesty, sent on the occasion of her Diamond Jubilee were much appreciated and I enclose a special message of thanks from The Queen, in return.

Yours sincerely,

Mrs. Sonia Bonici
Senior Correspondence Officer

Mr. Michael Davies and Ms. Fiona Lazenby.

25

 The thought of children, at any time but particularly at this time of year to be unaware of families, Christmas or the joy, meaning, happiness, fun, and smiles due to reasons or circumstances beyond their control, frankly, makes me sad and emotional."

Mike's 'Call to Arms' Email
December 2009

**ubject:** Real Social Benefits from Principle People.

I make no excuses for sending this to you late on a Thursday evening!

No, I have not been adversely affected by excess pharmaceuticals.

No, I have not been drinking.

No, I have not lost my sanity.

I want to share something with an important team of people whom I believe will understand and I hope will share my views on something and buy into a vision and an idea I have and want to develop.

Forgive my sentiments, but I have for many years had a desire to be in a position to help, through business, and increasingly personally, others less fortunate than my/ourselves in some way.

Primarily, to help those who are not in a position to help themselves, namely 'children'.

I have in the past had discussions with Phil and Andrew about my desire to assist in orphanages in Romania or somewhere.

The thought of children, at any time but particularly at this time of year to be unaware of families, Christmas or the joy, meaning, happiness, fun, and smiles due to reasons or circumstances beyond their control, frankly, makes me sad and emotional.

So, I have decided that in 2010 I want Principle Healthcare International (Group) to set something up and do something aimed at benefitting children in some way.

Not just to contribute to The Jo Jo Appeal, or send vitamins to third world countries, or to make donations to Children in Need etc, but to do something of a serious material nature which will cost time, money, and provide real benefit to children somewhere, somehow.

I want the healthcare element of our business to mean literally "healthcare" and relate it to children. Precisely what it will/could be is for discussion.

I think it should be something in the UK, maybe somewhere in Yorkshire, maybe funding/building a hostel/ day centre(s) for parents and kids to go and have fun, food, and warmth.

There must be many things it could be, but one thing is for sure... it will definitely be something, of that I am certain.

What do I want from you?

To think about this, and to let me know what you think, and whether in some way you are prepared to give a very small amount of time in work to 'Principle Kids'. Not very original but you understand the sentiment. It will not get in the way of our business but perhaps give more meaning to our developments, stresses, earnings, and time.

As a matter of good business practice, I do believe we should have a 'social responsibility' for the community, and I for one cannot think of a better or more worthy cause than "children".

The world in which children are going to grow up into is going to be difficult enough, but for some it will be much worse. I want to help in some small way.

We were all one once, some of us still are, some of us have, and all of us care.

As the saying goes… JFDI.

Are you with me?

Mike

Rationale Behind The Charity And How We Went About It

any people throughout the last 10 years have asked me: "why did I develop a charity, and what made me do it?".

The answer is always the same, it is simple, and straightforward and has two answers.

One is derived directly from my personal experience during my upbringing from 5 years old since losing my Mum. There is absolutely no doubt that I consider myself on reflection as having an 'underprivileged and disadvantaged' upbringing, which is one that I never want another child to suffer or live through. If there is anything I could do to help and assist other children in similar situations, then I would want to. I know only too well what it is like growing up in an environment which is, through tragic circumstances, difficult, and unhappy. Obviously, there are other situations which affect children in their formative years, not solely due to the loss of a parent. Many children are adopted, are in care, and maybe do not know their parents, only have one parent, live in poverty, are with foster parents, and many other distressful situations. Thus, my personal desire for a number of years has been to consider helping such children and families.

The other reason for developing the charity was driven by the businesses I had developed. By 2011 the Principle Group consisted of three separate companies, employing circa 150 people, developing and selling products to circa 50 countries around the world, with a turnover of circa £25 million. This group of companies did not have a written, and measured CSR policy. CSR standing for "Corporate Social Responsibility" policy.

Yes, the group operated ethically and had regular ethical audits to ensure compliance. Yes, the group operated with an environmental policy and tried to develop environmental sustainability in all areas of its operations. Yes, the group in UK held Investors in People Standard. All these areas were an integral part of good management practice. Yes, we had contributed to Children in Need, and sent vitamins via The International Aid Trust to needy people in poor countries. But we did not have a written CSR policy which not only involved these elements but also the key issue of a social strategy and being involved in the community, encouraging volunteering among the workforce, and contributing financially to charities and events. Thus, I considered that this strategy, coupled with my personal desire to help children and families could be a way to combine both the personal and the business opportunity and to develop our own charity to help children. I also believed that a coherent CSR policy, would mean more to current and new employees, likewise as the group grew in the future organically and maybe by acquisition, our integrated CSR policy would be positively received.

Having read a great deal about CSR in business I was convinced that this development would enhance the values of the business and encourage employees (and their families) to become more involved in the community by helping children in some way. The literature on CSR states that companies contribute to charities, employees have a responsibility to encourage social good within the company, customers are more likely to trade with a company with a clear CSR as they are more ethical, and a specific issue for me was "some company founders are also motivated to engage in CSR due to their personal convictions". It appeared to me that the only real element missing from CSR in our group was the social element. Decision made, let's get on with developing our own charity!

A charity would also add to my knowledge, experience, and skills and provide me with a long-term opportunity for an interest and a worthy hobby to manage, be involved in, and grow a charity.

The timing of this was also opportune! I would reach the tender young age of 60 years old on 5th January 2011, people and relatives had been asking what I wanted for my birthday milestone. The answer became clear! Personally, I do not want anything, other than for people to contribute to this "unnamed, yet to be developed charity!".

These are the reasons why the charity was thought of. Opportunity and timing were coincidental, but right!

My email to key managers in the group was sent after I had watched an episode of DIY SOS on the TV. It was all about a family with five young children in North Wales, all living with their mum and dad in a caravan on the site of a derelict house, which the dad was re-building for the family. During the time of the building process, the mum became ill and sadly died, leaving the dad and five kids in a cramped caravan. There was no time for the dad to continue the build as he had to be both mum and dad to his five kids. Then DIY SOS heard of the plight, and Nick Knowles and the team arrived to rebuild the derelict home for all the family. What a difference to the family, no mum but a home they were all excited about. The smiles on the kids' faces said everything. Both my wife and I were in tears watching the TV programme. This was the "point of action". My email was sent late at night. Every recipient said "yes, let's do it!".

Selecting the people to help me was easy! Nicky Midgley was my Personal Assistant and had been involved in the thought process thus far. Fiona Lazenby had family and friend experience of this. Clare Campbell and I had worked together for 15 years in two companies, and she had relevant skills and experience. All three ladies became Trustees and helped form the start of the charity.

The name was selected The Principle Trust Charity. Registered at Charity Commission and Companies House.

What precisely would the charity do? Involvement with children "yes", but what?!

We thought of money for orphanages in Romania, schools in villages in Africa, and activities for children in need.

We all agreed that it should be something in the UK maybe Yorkshire, where we, employees, family, and volunteers, could be near to and see, help, and assist. Maybe funding a building or day centre for children to visit and have warmth, food, and fun? We needed to get to a focal point and tried to find people who maybe could help us get to it.

There are people or consultants who will do work to assist at a crazy daily rate of ££ pay! No thanks, we want the money for the charity.

We contacted the church, our local MP, special need schools, and the local council. Everyone was really excited to hear our plans and obviously wanted us to support their ideas. Including building and then running a community centre in Skipton, employing staff to run it, and a chef to make the food etc... Quite a project and quite a cost! Way above our thoughts. We believed that we would just be substituting what the council or government should be doing so declined the offer!

Then we got somewhere. Craven Council suggested very helpfully that we should contact a man in North Yorkshire Social Services. They put us in touch with Mr Karl Podmore who came to visit us along with one of his staff.

His story, data, locations, and ideas brought us to a focus point. We were nearly there!

Our logo from the early years, supporting underprivileged and disadvantaged children.

The Principle Trust

Helping children have a holiday

Karl Podmore, Disabled Children's Service Manager - North Yorkshire County Council

ike and Trustees (Clare, Fiona, and Nicky) being based in Skipton North Yorkshire, knew they wanted to help children and establish a charity but did not have a clear direction on which children, where, how, or why.

They met with a number of people to discuss what could be done and some consultants charging high daily rates of pay for advice and proposals. The latter being declined as the money would be better spent towards the children!

Following conversations with Craven District Council it was proposed that they would make contact with North Yorkshire County Council (NYCC) to find out whether there would be anyone able to help and assist them with their desire to help children.

Karl Podmore General Manager in the Children and Young People's Service based in Northallerton received a message to see if he could offer advice to Mike and his fellow Trustees. He arranged a meeting with Nicky and the Charity Team in Skipton to find out more and see whether he could help and assist.

Karl visited Skipton with a colleague from the Disabled Children's Service and met with the team on 12th August 2010 - he remembers this clearly because it was his birthday!

He outlined his role, and the breadth of services which his area provided. He made a presentation to the team describing the numbers, and diverse needs of the children the Council worked with. This included the numbers of children looked after in care, those in need of safeguarding, and a large number of children in need, either through being disabled, vulnerable, young carers, or living with families experiencing disadvantage. He talked about the challenges some families experienced around poor housing, domestic abuse, and substance misuse. It was highlighted that the number of children known to Social Workers was only a tiny percentage of all children living in North Yorkshire but there were families living very difficult lives and who would benefit from help and assistance.

Several ideas were discussed about how the charity could help and assist the children and families Karl had described. Karl is a Trustee, on behalf of the council, for a well-established charity in North Yorkshire and County Durham which gave practical assistance to people in recovery or living in poverty, including the provision of holidays.

Holidays became a focal point of the discussion as it was identified that many of the children Karl described had never been on a holiday, thus enjoying all the resultant benefits that holidays give. Families living on low incomes, living with abuse, debt, or substance misuse were unlikely to have the possibility to go on holiday.

A holiday home in the Yorkshire Dales was suggested as a holiday venue, which would have been a good idea but many of the children living in North Yorkshire do live close to the countryside. What many of the children do not see (apart from those living on the coast) is the seaside. Scarborough, Southport, and Blackpool were all considered as possible venues with Blackpool being the preferred location due to its popularity as a UK holiday destination, with amenities, activities, and relatively accessible to North Yorkshire by road or rail.

We did agree at this stage that the charity would not consider holiday homes specifically adapted for disabled children, but it was a longer-term ambition for the charity if its model proved to be a success.

The Trustees accepted responsibility to go and check out locations in the Blackpool area, the potential sites for holiday homes and consider the costs and suitability for the children and families that we were thinking of.

Karl agreed to establish a new process within his service for Social Workers to be briefed about the opportunity for families and children to be considered for a free holiday and to establish a straightforward communication process between NYCC and the Charity for bookings.

Karl visited the two holiday homes that the charity selected, which were luxury static caravans on the Haven Holiday Park in Marton Mere near Blackpool. They were 6 berths, with 3 bedrooms, suitably fitted and kitted out by the Charity for the whole process to commence. Haven Holiday Park is open from Easter to Bonfire Night in November, for around 33 weeks a year. With two caravans the charity would start the holiday process with up to 66 weeks available for children and families to benefit from free holidays they otherwise may not have had.

Karl has remained in touch with the Trust throughout the last ten years and we have kept him up to date with the successful expansion of both the charity and the number of holiday homes available. The referral process, allocation, and administration of bookings has altered but the relationship has developed. As Karl's role changed to managing the Council's Disabled Children's Service the charity echoed this by having accessible facilities to enable disabled children and their families to take advantage of having a holiday by the sea or in a lodge in the countryside.

Why Holidays?

Several different ideas were discussed with Karl Podmore at North Yorkshire County Council about how the charity could potentially support and help children and their families.

Holidays became a focal point of the discussion as it was identified that many of the children Karl described had never been on a holiday, thus enjoying all the resultant benefits that holidays could give. The Council had already identified diverse needs of the children throughout the area. This included some children looked after in care, those in need of safeguarding, and a large number of children in need, either through being disabled, vulnerable, young carers, or living with families experiencing disadvantage. It was also highlighted that families living on low incomes, living with abuse, debt, or substance misuse were very unlikely to have the opportunity to be able to afford to go on holiday as a family.

The charity then came across the insightful work of Dr Margot Sunderland, an award-winning author and child mental health expert. She explains that 'As adults, we countdown to our summer holidays to recharge our batteries. But they can also be a profoundly beneficial time for children. Parents are focused not on work, but on play, thereby giving their children the prized gift of time.'

Dr Sunderland's scientific and psychological research on the long-term impact of adult/child relationships on the child's developing brain and mind, particularly what she had to say about holidays and the benefits this brought to the adult/child relationship was very thought provoking and further cemented the idea of The Principle Trust Children's Charity providing free holidays to underprivileged and disadvantaged children.

We learned from Dr Sunderland's books and articles in the press that what is less widely known is that holidays can also advance brain development in children. So, when you take your child on a holiday, you are supporting their explorative urge (SEEKING system) a vital resource for living life well, and their capacity to play (PLAY system). In adulthood, this translates into the ability to play with ideas, essential, for example, to the successful entrepreneur.

After this extensive research and discussions with local authorities our aims for the charity became clear to us, and helped us to form our aims and objectives:

"The main objects of The Principle Trust is the prevention or relief of poverty in Yorkshire by providing grants or items or services to individuals in need and/or charities or other organizations working to prevent or relieve poverty.

The purpose is the relief of those in need by reason of youth, age, ill health, disability, financial hardship, or other disadvantage.

The above object and purpose will be achieved by The Principle Trust via the provision of holiday homes for those in need, providing the opportunity of a holiday that otherwise would not be possible."

Haven Marton Mere Holiday Village, Blackpool.

Development Of The Charity
And Our Holiday Homes

One of the luxury caravans at
Marton Mere, Blackpool.

A team building day at Marton Mere, Blackpool.

Interior of one of the luxury caravans at Marton Mere, Blackpool.

Log cabin at Ribblesdale Park, Gisburn.

The lodge at Parkdean White Cross Bay Holiday park, Windermere.

Our first two luxury caravans were purchased in early 2011, ready for the Haven Holiday Park season opening at the end of March 2011. This was when we would start offering free holidays to underprivileged and disadvantaged children.

We specifically did not include "disabled children holidays" at this stage primarily due to the fact that the caravans were not suitably equipped for receiving disabled children.

The uptake on free holidays was remarkable. We were oversubscribed during the first few years and were disappointed to have to refuse children a holiday due to all the holiday weeks being allocated. There can be a variety of different situations which affect underprivileged and disadvantaged children, not solely due to the loss of a parent. Many children are adopted, are in care, and maybe do not know their parents, only have one parent, live in poverty, are with foster parents, and many other distressful situations.

We had to set about fundraising to bring in money to the charity to not only pay the bills, but to try and raise sufficient money to consider purchasing another holiday home to enable even more children to have holidays.

In addition to developing events to fundraise, we set about applying to organisations for grants and awards for our charity. This was successful and we were soon raising more than we needed to run and manage the two holiday homes. By 2014 we had raised sufficient money to purchase another holiday home at Haven Holiday

Park thus then we had three homes.

This meant that we were able to offer about 99 weeks of free holidays per year. We had three homes, and the holiday park was open for 33 weeks for their season. This was good news, and we were soon filling 99 weeks per season.

However, this also meant that we needed to raise even more money in fundraising to run three holiday homes. Each holiday home costs us around £10,000 per season to run. This amount is made up of Haven ground rent, insurance, all utilities (water/gas/electric/rates) plus cleaning, maintenance, repairs, season clean downs and drainage. Thus, we had to raise £30,000 per annum just to cover the running costs. Of course, damages, and wear and tear occur quite frequently which all adds cost. So, in order to achieve any further holiday homes, we knew we had to raise well above the £30,000 per annum which we needed just to cover costs.

By 2017 we were raising more than £30,000 per annum so started saving up for our next holiday home. The question was "where, whom for, and why?".

The Trustees and some Partners got together to review the data relating to disabled children and children living with adversity in Yorkshire. We were staggered at the number of children classed as disabled. Far more than we ever imagined. Maybe this was a route to our next holiday home? A disabled home?

The Trustees began considering what was necessary and where would make sense for a disabled home. It was agreed that peace and quiet, open spaces, suitably equipped lodge, or home with disabled access i.e. ramp, wide doors for wheelchairs, profiling bed, electric hoist for mobility, wet room, or space for wheelchair in bathroom, lack of noise, flat landscape for wheelchair use, and nice walks. These were criteria chosen by Partners whom would be involved in using the disabled facility.

We used the word "disability" but in reality, we include those that are living with adversity because of life threatening illness, life limiting illness, respite care, autism, hearing or vision impaired, Down's syndrome, cystic fibrosis, recovering from serious injury or illness, to name a few. We selected several sites and visited many. Many were ideal but were on a hillside, some were too remote and inaccessible, but the one we chose was Ribblesdale Park in Gisburn, 15 miles from Skipton. Beautiful countryside setting, lovely walks, and to top it off it has a hot tub on the decking which has proved to be a real hit with families.

The lodge is excellent, wooden floors are ideal for wheelchairs, and we made amends to the lodge for full access for disabled families. Yes, it is a very quiet location, with limited public transport therefore personal transport is necessary.

We opened the lodge in June 2018 and have had a vast cross section of children and families staying. A few have commented that it is quiet with little to do, hence the need for transport to get out and about. But we chose somewhere quiet by design. We have had many mini breaks of families staying there as they have been unsure whether their child would cope with a whole week away. Most have been really appreciative of the free holiday, with lots of lovely testimonials. The Gisburn site is open for 52 weeks per year so we have an opportunity to add 52 weeks to our 99 weeks available in our three Blackpool based caravans.

But it means that we now must raise £40,000 per annum to cover the costs of running 4 homes!

The charity likes a challenge, and really started to spend time on raising funds towards another disabled home (after raising £40k to run four of them). We were successful during the latter part of 2018 and 2019 in raising funds for another home. We were grossly over subscribed for the disabled home so decided on another one! This time we looked towards the Lake District and found an ideal location at Parkdean White Cross Bay Holiday Park, 2 miles outside Windermere and on the edge of the lake. We purchased a lodge, slightly smaller than Gisburn, and set about totally renovating it to be suitable for disabled children. No external hot tub at this stage but the finished lodge all renovated looked fantastic. We have had partners come and view it, and it was formally opened in February 2020.

Regrettably after just four visits from families to the home along came the COVID-19 pandemic and national lockdown! So, we have yet to have the real full benefit of five holiday homes operating and running with families and children benefitting from them.

" The holiday had made a world of difference to her and her daughter, that helped put the bad memories of the past behind them."

Stories From Underprivileged And Disadvantaged Children And Their Families

Anne and Emily's' Story

We always try and insist that all free holidays we give are recommended to us by a third-party organisation such as social workers, the church, local council, schools, other charities, hospitals, and other such organisations. Occasionally we would receive a request directly from the person wanting a holiday. In these circumstances, particularly if the request is verbal, we ask for the request in writing, along with any details of someone whom we can speak to in order that we can validate the story and the request.

The follow up to a request on the telephone was a five-page handwritten letter on A4 paper. The lady whom wrote the letter, called Anne, had a seven year old daughter called Emily. Anne explained how Emily was a carefree, happy young girl, with lots of friends, helpful to her mum, always smiling, and helping others. She loved singing and music. In many ways she was a model pupil at school.

Anne and Emily had recently moved from the South of England, upon recommendation from Social Services to get away from their troubled life where they lived previously.

Their first letter to the charity told a very harrowing story of how both Anne and Emily had lived with Emily's Dad who became violent and abusive to both his partner Anne and his daughter Emily. They lived in fear of him having had too much to drink and becoming hurtful towards them. He would hurt them and be spiteful to them in many ways. His violence towards Anne was unprovoked, shouting, vulgar, hitting, causing bruises, and hurt to the mum. When Emily became involved and told him to stop, he turned his anger on to Emily and would slap and kick her, grab her arms, and put her in her bedroom and lock the door.

This abuse went on for many months with neither Anne nor Emily saying anything to anyone. They were too frightened to say anything as he would hit them even more.

One day Emily was at school and her teacher noticed how withdrawn she had become, she had noticed how her happy personality had changed, and saw what she thought were bruises on her arms and legs. She alerted Social Services who came to the school along with Emily's Mum for a discussion. Both Emily and Anne broke down in tears and relayed the story of systematic abuse over a long time. The extent of Anne's injuries required her to attend hospital, although both Anne and Emily lived in fear of what the actions would be by Anne's partner when he knew about the development.

The police were alerted and took the partner for questioning. He eventually admitted the hurt and harm caused to the mum and his daughter. He was arrested, found guilty of grievous bodily harm, and sent to prison.

Anne and Emily were very pleased for the respite but worried that he would continue the harm once released from prison. Thus, Anne and Emily relocated to a new home in Lancashire, very close to The Principle Trust Children's Charity.

Clearly this was a story which requires the charity to help and offer a holiday and break away. Particularly as Anne stated that her, nor Emily had ever been on a holiday together. The charity spoke to Anne who agreed to arrange for Social Services to send a recommendation for her and Emily to have a free holiday. It was agreed that Anne and Emily would go to Blackpool into one of the caravans on the Haven Holiday Park. They were delighted, happy, and really looked forward to the holiday. The charity arranged for some toys and games and suggested some trips they might like to take when in Blackpool. Off they went to Blackpool for their holiday.

The next time the charity heard from them was during the week after they returned. There was a telephone call from Anne, sounding so happy (she said she was "giddy") with thanks to everyone for allowing her and Emily to have the holiday. She said that Emily had smiled from long before they went to Blackpool, all the time they were there, and had not stopped talking about it since they came back to their new home. Emily made lots of friends, played on all the rides, went swimming in the pool every day, even in the rain! She went exploring everywhere with her new friends, spent time in other caravans playing with children, and other children came to Emily's caravan to play. Anne was so relieved and pleased to see her happy daughter reliving her happy times, laughing, smiling, and being very happy, and free from the trauma of the recent past. Anne said that not only was Emily looking forward to her new life, in a new location, with new school and new friends, but Anne firmly believed that she was at last free of the hurt and harm her ex-partner had caused.

Anne was in no doubt that both her and Emily's mental health had improved dramatically, their sense of wellbeing, trust and hope for the future had improved significantly and they were both looking forward to better days ahead with optimism and without fear! She said that the holiday had made a world of difference to her and her daughter, that helped put the bad memories of the past behind them.

The charity likes to receive phone calls and letters with positive feedback!

'Karen and Alex's' Story

We came to hear about Karen and Alex's family through Embrace, a very special charity, who support children and families who are victims of serious crime. We learnt about Alex, a 10-year-old boy whose mother was brutally murdered by her partner.

Alex's family rallied around him and he had been taken into the care of his Auntie Karen who along with her own children was heavily overtaken with grief. Despite the care being given, the location of the tragic event was very nearby, and due to living in a small, tight knit community, Alex and his immediate family were faced daily with constant reminders of his mother and the very tragic circumstances of her death.

We agreed to help Alex and his Auntie and her children. We felt a holiday with his family would be a way to remind Alex that it was OK to once again be a child, to enjoy himself without fear of consequence and to bring back a degree of normality to what was and again will be a bright, caring, and fun-natured 10-year-old boy.

The week after the family had holidayed at Blackpool we received a letter from Karen and Alex's Family Liaison Officer in the police. The officer explained that they wanted to thank The Principle Trust personally! High praise indeed. They were in regular contact with them had seen first-hand a noticeable improvement in Alex. Although the family were sceptical about being "seen" to enjoy themselves in the wake of his mum's murder, they felt the holiday at Marton Mere was just what they needed.

The holiday brought the boy's new immediate family together as one. This short but well-needed break showed them, more importantly Alex, that despite the tragic circumstances that have brought them together as a core family unit, they can ensure he has age-appropriate fun and enjoyment, along with giving themselves satisfaction that they are able to care for and nurture the 10-year-old as if he were their own. It was a tonic for all who attended and a comfort to the extended family that Alex was having what the family described as the "time of his life".

Spending time together as a family away from the constant reminders of what had happened, coming together, and having a great time without feeling guilty for smiling again without a doubt helped them to bond and start to look towards their future.

'The Thompson' Family Story

We work closely with organisations like local councils, social workers, and other charities who then recommend children and their families who would really benefit from a free holiday. Making Space is one of our partners, and they have seen first-hand what a big difference a holiday can make to the children and families they support.

The charity received a request for a holiday via the charity Making Space, they told us of the Thompson family, and how the child's mum cared for her husband who suffered badly from a painful condition called fibromyalgia. Caring for a family member or loved one is a very generous and selfless thing to do and it can be extremely rewarding. However, taking on such a physically and emotionally demanding role can also take its toll on family life, especially so whilst bringing up a toddler who has complex health problems.

The Thompson family desperately needed a break away from daily life and caring responsibilities and we could understand the stress and pressures of being a carer, the constant worry and feeling of isolation. We just had to help, and the family were put forwards for a holiday in Blackpool at one of our caravans.

We very much enjoyed hearing from the family after they got back from their time away. In their letter they said – "We would like to say thank you so very much, we really appreciate you giving us this opportunity for a 7-night family holiday on a fantastic site that all of us would love to visit again, giving us a chance to relax and distress at a pace we choose, giving us time away from day-to-day life. It has allowed our two-year-old to be a child and build childhood memories in turn, allowing mummy and daddy to relax seeing our son get a lot out of this. It was just great to get away as a family and we were able to do this at minimal expense. Holidays are not something we can afford to do, in fact our holiday in Blackpool was our first family holiday together. From the bottom of our hearts thank you!".

The mum went on to tell us that she felt an immediate positive impact when they all returned home. "It was amazing having a few days off and escaping from stress and having memories to look back on. When you are dealing with so much in your life a holiday is so important for your mental health and wellbeing".

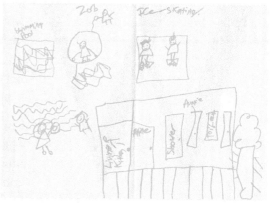

'The Jones' Family Story

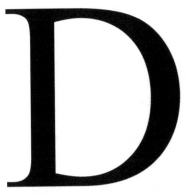iane Watts works for The Embrace Charity whom help Child Victims of Crime (CVOC). This does not mean those children whom have committed a crime but those whom are the Victims of Crime against them. Diane has become a great friend and supporter of our charity, as she knows what a difference a free holiday can make to the children and their families whom have been affected by criminal acts.

Equally our charity likes to help Embrace as much as possible as we can see and hear about the real, meaningful difference a free holiday can make to the family.

The Jones family is such a story.

Mrs Jones and her two children had lived with an abusing husband and father to her and her children for a long time. The children were badly affected by the abuse which the father inflicted on them. Mrs Jones, in attempting to protect the children was badly abused. They were both physically and mentally affected by the actions. Ultimately the police became involved and the father was found guilty and was sent to prison for his actions.

However, the family lived in fear of his release and the abuse and violence starting all over again.

Diane had been in contact with the family, and before confirming anything to them she discussed with us whether the family could go on a week's break to a caravan. For three reasons:

They had never been away on a holiday as a family before.

To obtain some respite from the situation in a nicer environment.

To consider and plan as a family what they wanted to do when the father was released from prison.

Naturally, we readily agreed to them going on holiday and we fixed a week. Diane took them to Blackpool, and also purchased for them some tickets to go to Madame Tussauds Museum.

When Mrs Jones was told of the holiday by Diane, she readily agreed to go but thought that she and the children would just stay on the holiday park, near the caravan and be in their comfort zone as she knew they would be safe there.

Mrs Jones called us after the holiday and told us of her and the children experience during the weeks holiday.

She said: "We had a really great time at the caravan, it was lovely, it was really special for us, and made us feel safe and secure. We were able to go out and enjoy the park, the beach, and Madame Tussauds was really interesting, seeing models of people we had only seen on TV and in books and magazines, it was fun. Me and the children were able to sit in comfort, relax, and talk about the future and what we wanted to happen to our lives. We did not, under any circumstances want to go back to the same house and suffer again when he was released from prison. The holiday and the park, and time together made us realise that we wanted a different life from all the abuse. We decided we wanted to move from the family home, but not so far that the children would have to change schools and lose all their friends. We decided that we did not want to live in a refuge, as we were not to blame for these abusive actions it was my husband and children's father. It was his fault we lived in fear.

The holiday, the caravan, and the whole experience made us so much happier and safe as a family, and that was the feeling we wanted to keep for the future.

The week of safety gave us and the children the confidence and strength to make the break from the old abusive life and make a new happier life elsewhere.

Mrs Jones went on to say that she made plans whilst at the caravan, to be relocated some distance away from where they previously lived, and they will be rehomed. Her final comments to us were that this holiday was the best thing you or anyone has ever done for us and now we have a very positive attitude and the confidence to make a better life.

Thank you so much for giving us a brilliant holiday and making us stronger as a family".

Diane also contacted us after speaking with Mrs Jones after the family had returned from the holiday. Diane said that she was a different person. So much happier, confident, positive, and ready to face the future in a different location, without the historic abuse, and wanted to thank the Charity once again for giving her and her children the holiday which has helped them renew their lives.

Mavis' Family Story

Just sometimes a chance meeting or connection between people results in a wonderful story and a free holiday from our charity which really helps exactly the right people in very different and difficult circumstances.

The story of Mavis and her family is such a story.

Pauline and Rodney Doyle are great friends and supporters of our charity. They happened to be on holiday themselves and met Janet Town, whom lives near Leeds and is actively involved in her local church. In discussions Janet happened to relay to Pauline a story about a family.

Janet says Mavis, her husband, and four children came to UK from Ghana to start a new life. The family had suffered in silence at the hands of their father for two years, and in the UK he had tried to trick the mother in to signing papers which gave him custody of the children. The mother did not sign the papers, and eventually the father left the family and returned to Ghana. This left Mavis and her four children with absolutely nothing. Janet explained that her church had helped and assisted as much as it was able in providing clothes, some furniture, food, and help. The situation was awful and almost unimaginable. Mother and four children left with nothing in a new country.

Upon hearing the story, the Charity readily agreed that it would provide a holiday in Blackpool for the family.

The church arranged transport for the family to get to Haven Holiday Park.

We had a discussion with Blackpool Zoo and explained the situation of the family and very generously they provided free tickets for them to visit the zoo.

This story had a real effect on me personally, and I arranged a Haven credit card with money on for Mavis and the family to use during their week on food, restaurants, entertainment, and refreshments etc…

We received a note from Mavis after her holiday with

the children, saying:

"The offer of a free holiday for us came at exactly the right time. I was very down with no hope for me and my children. The Charity put smiles on our faces. The holiday was the first one the children and I had experienced in our life, and the voucher we were given to spend, and being able to experience eating out together as a family in a restaurant was amazing. Being able to visit the zoo and for the children to see the wild animals was also a first for the children. We all really enjoyed the holiday and to enjoy the food, entertainment, and gifts was an overwhelming experience.

There are so many first-time experiences that The Principle Trust have provided for us as a family. Thank you."

Hearing of this wonderful family, had us arrange also for them to visit Santa's Grotto at Christmas and provide them with gifts. They had to travel on a train to get there which was also a first-time experience for them. Once again, I provided Mavis with a Marks and Spencer gift card to buy her and the children some Christmas gifts. This brings so much happiness to such a wonderful family.

I had the pleasure of meeting Mavis and her lovely kids at Christmas. What a lovely family. Big smiles and laughter, fun and jokes. I am personally delighted that we are involved as a charity with this family.

'Tony and Julie's' Story

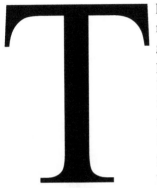The Charity received a holiday request from a Social Worker in the Bradford area requesting that Tony (the dad) and his daughter Julie who was 6 years old could go for a holiday to the Blackpool caravan. The background was that 8 months previously Julie's Mum and Tony's wife Helen had died from cancer. Social Services believed that Tony and Julie would really benefit from the holiday, and it would give them something positive to look forward to. The request was also for Helen's Mum and Dad (Julie's Grandparents) to go with them on holiday, as it would benefit them to be with their granddaughter and see her having fun. The previous 8 months had been a really difficult time for Tony, balancing going to work with looking after Julie. The grandparents lived at the other side of the country to Tony and Julie, so did not get to see their granddaughter very often as they lived so far away. Unfortunately, Tony's parents had both passed away, so Helen's Mum and Dad were Julie's only grandparents.

The charity agreed for the family to go to a caravan in Blackpool. The follow up and feedback we got from the grandparents after the holiday was lovely.

Julie spent time every day in the swimming pool with her dad, and he taught her to swim properly. He also taught her to dive in and swim underwater. The grandparents explained that seeing Julie so happy, doing so many things like enjoying the playgrounds, going on the swings, going to Blackpool Zoo, and seeing many animals she had never seen before, she particularly liked the Sea Lions. Going to the beach and riding a donkey, burying her dad in the sand. She preferred the swimming pool to the sea, as the sea was too cold! She and her dad went to The Sandcastle which is a massive indoor swimming pool complex with slides, fountains, wave machines, water chutes, and she had a great time with her dad.

The grandparents enjoyed spending holiday time with their son-in-law and Julie and mentioned how well they bonded and got on. This was a perfect holiday to help Julie and Tony be together and have some smiles and fun. It would never make up for the loss of Helen, but it helped make happy memories.

The follow up letter proved to us that what we were doing offering children, whom for whatever reason were underprivileged or disadvantaged a free holiday was right. However, what we were not prepared for at all was another letter we received from the grandparents just some six weeks later.

Julie's dad Tony had suffered a major heart attack and sadly passed away. Life is just not fair. For Julie to have lost her mum to cancer, then within 10 months to lose her dad to a heart attack is unimaginable. The grandparents said that Julie had now gone to live them, as she has no other relatives or grandparents near to where she lived in Yorkshire. They were doing their best to make the adjustment for her, and trying to help her in her new school, make new friends, and do their best to help her.

They were at pains to say how Julie kept talking about the time she and her dad had spent at Blackpool, how she remembered the swimming, the zoo, the sand, and having a great time with her dad. The grandparents were just so grateful that Julie had these special memories to cherish of her holiday with her dad at Blackpool, thanks to The Principle Trust Charity.

Ethan's Story

We first came to hear about a little boy named Ethan after an introduction to his mum whilst at a children's training session at a local cricket club. Ethan's mum began to tell us how back in October 2012, her family received the most shocking and devasting news. Ethan, their beloved son had been diagnosed with leukaemia after having been seriously unwell. She explained that leukaemia is a very serious illness, it is a type of cancer that affects the bodies white blood cells and its these cells that help our bodies fight infections.

She went on to recount how the whole family was utterly heartbroken, devasted by the news, and very scared about what we would happen to Ethan. Their positive mindset of 'right then, let's crack on with it' really helped the family to get through the worst of times whilst Ethan received his treatment in hospital. She said that everyone in their local community was absolutely great, very helpful, and caring to all their family, which was really touching and helped them to get through the difficult time together. It was a very tough time for all of them.

When Ethan was well enough and had completed his specialist treatment, we gave him and his family a chance to go on holiday for free to our caravan at Haven Holiday Park in Blackpool. We felt the family had been through so much and would really benefit from some time away to escape the worry, have fun together, and make some precious memories together as a family unit.

After they came back from their weeklong stay at Blackpool, the family got in touch with us at the Charity to tell us about their holiday and what a great time they had had altogether after such a difficult few years, whilst their little boy was battling the serious illness. His mum told us the holiday resort was fantastic, the caravan was lovely, and it had everything they could possibly need. She mentioned the free bus available too, which they would catch to get into Blackpool itself, allowing them to experience all the sights and sounds of the seaside town, and all it had to offer. We were delighted that the family had such a fantastic time together and made lots of memories. At the holiday park there is adventure golf, a soft play area, family shows, live music in the evening, and other entertainment which the family enjoyed. We loved hearing from Ethan's mum that "the evening entertainment was brilliant, the kids loved it! We are so very grateful that we were given the chance from The Principle Trust of going to such a lovely place together."

Everyone at the Charity enjoys hearing the children's tales about their stay whilst at our holiday homes. We get sent lots of lovely thank you letters through the post, emails with photographs attached of children having fun, with big smiles on their faces building sandcastles on the beach, and some very arty drawings too! This is what makes what we do worthwhile and makes us more determined than ever to help more children in similar circumstances whether that be through ill health, complex disabilities, or those who are disadvantaged and underprivileged who may never have had experienced a family holiday before.

Family referred by IDAS

A specialist charity in Yorkshire supporting anyone experiencing
or affected by domestic abuse or sexual violence.

he Charity was contacted by Maureen from IDAS which is a charity based in Yorkshire whom offer help and assistance to victims of violence or sexual abuse.

Maureen explained that IDAS was providing help and support to a mother and daughter aged 6 years old. The mother also had a son of 12 years old. The mother and two children had been the victims of both physical and sexual abuse by the father. Particularly when he had been drinking too much alcohol.

The police had got involved as the mother could not take any more beatings, nor allow her children to witness the suffering. The father was also violent towards the children which was reported to Social Services by their schools.

The 12-year-old son had gone to live with his grandparents as he was at a secondary school some way beyond the family home. His mother could not get her daughter to primary school in the morning, and her son to secondary school in time for lessons. Thus, the grandparents agreed for her son to live with them. The mum and daughter only saw the son at weekends, and the close-knit family being split up was not ideal. Living apart was having an effect on all 3 people and causing lot of upset and distress.

Maureen from IDAS wondered whether the family qualified for a family holiday all together for a week. We naturally agreed, as this was exactly why the charity exists to help children and families such as this.

We agreed the week availability with Maureen, and the mum wanted us to confirm that we would not tell her husband where they were if he were to contact us. The mum and two children did not want any further contact with him, and they were awaiting a court order to stop him contacting them.

The family went to Blackpool. We received a letter from the son two weeks before they went to say how excited he was to be spending a week away with his mum and sister, and how kind it was of us to arrange this for them. How much he was looking forward to them being a family again!

They contacted the Charity during their stay at Blackpool to say how much they were enjoying themselves, being together as a family, and free from worry about the father coming home drunk. They told us they had been in swimming and on the water chutes in the pool every day. They had a really good time in the entertainment lounge in the evenings. They had been to Blackpool Zoo, and even in the Blackpool rain had really enjoyed themselves. They said they would let us know after their week away about the other things they had done.

The family sounded exactly as a family should. Excited, enjoying themselves, having fun, free from harm, exploring new things, and putting the family back together again as a loving unit. Exactly as planned, after the holiday we received not a letter, but a phone call from the mum, and Maureen was also present.

The mum was so overjoyed at the week with her family back together that she was very emotional and crying. So, Maureen took over the call and explained that the mum and daughter were absolutely full of stories about their week in Blackpool and had returned to IDAS with a new resolve to get another house or flat where all three of them could live together safely, away from the abusive father.

Maureen explained how grateful IDAS were to us for providing the holiday and giving the family hope, resolve, encouragement, unity, and a strong desire to start a new life for the three of them.

Mission accomplished by the Charity. It is stories such as this which give the charity and all the people the motivation to carry on and do even more good for other worthy children and their families.

Snippets Of Thanks From More Families Who Have Enjoyed Their Holidays

"We really needed this holiday to be ourselves again for a short while, and just to be able to put our family first.

We got to spend quality time with the children making precious memories. We have been having a difficult time at the moment and recently our little girl has been in hospital for a length of time, which was frightening and very stressful for all the family.

I was able to recharge my batteries and help bond better again with my daughter.

Thank you so much to all at The Principle Trust Children's Charity, I was overwhelmed with this holiday, the accommodation, the swimming pool area was amazing! It put a spring in my and my family's step again.

Once again, thank you."

"We'd resisted going into a refuge because why should we move when it's the father of my children who was to blame for us living in fear. But feeling so safe and happy together at the holiday home was a feeling we wanted to keep."

#OurYorkshireChildren

The Principle Trust
Children's Charity

making memories that last

"What a lovely experience we will always cherish, thank you so much!"

#OurYorkshireChildren

"As a result of extreme poverty, the child had never seen outside of their local community. This free break gave them an experience they could never forget."

#OurYorkshireChildren

Just a few words to say a big thank you to everybody at The Principle Trust for our family holiday.

Being a single parent to a child, booking a holiday can very daunting, as there are always other things that come up throughout the year which take priority. Being given a holiday this year through the Trust has given myself and my son a well-deserved break, which we wouldn't have had otherwise, so thank you.

The caravan we stay in had everything we needed, plus plenty of space to move around in. The site at Marton Mere was excellent too, having lots of activities for both of us to enjoy. My little boy particularly enjoyed a game of adventure golf each day, followed by a few hours in the splash area.

We took advantage of being in Blackpool and managed a trip to the zoo and an afternoon at Nickelodeon Land at the Pleasure Beach.

Once again, many thanks."

"The young people from the children's home really enjoyed the holiday. Thank you to everyone who support The Principle Trust."

#OurYorkshireChildren

"The holiday was to remind the child of the murdered mother, that it was ok to once again be a child and to enjoy themselves without fear of consequence."

#OurYorkshireChildren

"It is often the most vulnerable children who benefit from these holidays and they deserve to have something good happen in life and miss the chaos and adversity they often have to endure. And that is the biggest reason I think The Principle Trust is a fantastic charity."

#OurYorkshireChildren

"The day that a lady and two young girls turned up at the Charity offices and rang the doorbell. When the Charity lady answered the door, the lady, who was a single mum said that they had just returned the previous week from a holiday in Blackpool and had a wonderful time. She said that her two daughters had never been on a holiday before and did not know what to expect. The girls had loved every minute of it and at night they were so exhausted that they fell fast asleep straight away. The two girls had a thank you card for the Charity staff, which they had written themselves, and had a small box of chocolates each which they wanted to give to the Charity Staff to say "Thank You" for letting them go on holiday. A lovely touch for the mum coming to the charity and for the two girls whom had such a great time wanting to give a present to the staff!"

"There are lots of children who struggle as a result of their parents having mental health issues including self-harm and suicide."

#OurYorkshireChildren

"The holidays provide families caught in the hardship of life, the opportunity to lift the burdens of life for a short time and become refreshed which in turn enables them to parent more positively."

#OurYorkshireChildren

"The child was abducted and fortunately the car was stopped by the police. However, this did not prevent the perpetrator from physically abusing the child. A holiday for this child is not just a holiday, it's a safe place to go."

#OurYorkshireChildren

The Principle Trust
Children's Charity
making memories that last

Chris, the owner of Coastal Cleaning, whom looks after the Caravans in Blackpool often tells us stories about the families who stay there.

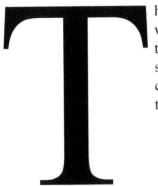

There was a family staying in a caravan with a son of 8 and a daughter of 11. They were having a great time and when Chris called at the caravan to check all was ok the two children ran up to him, hugged him, wanted to kiss him, and thanked him so much for letting them come and stay in his caravan. The kids thought that the cleaner was the owner of the caravan and were having such a fantastic time that they just wanted to hug him! According to Chris this was a regular occurrence!"

Stories From Disabled Families Who Have Visited Our Log Cabin and Lodge

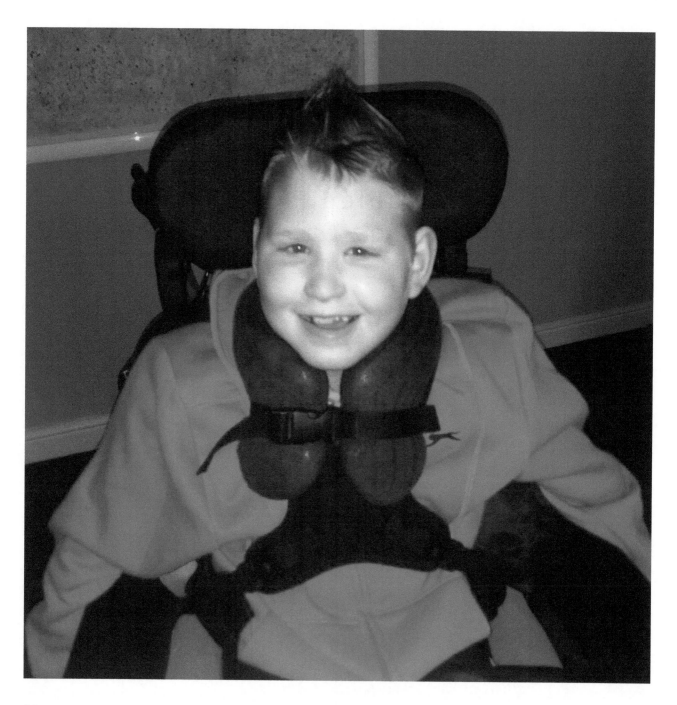

Toby's Family Story

Myself and Toby's dad separated when Toby was 3 years old and I met Toby's stepdad just before Toby turned 6 years old. The breakaway was well needed because we had been working on renovating the old house for 3 years so that we could sell it and move into our forever home. We currently live in a council adapted property. We have had lots of things go wrong lately and the house didn't sell like we expected, and we have actually had to take it to auction. All this has been very upsetting and stressful, and the break gave us something to look forward to. Having time to really relax and forget the stress was beneficial to all of us. Being away from all the chaos at home, really meant we could really relax for the first time in a long time.

Toby is a bright, cheerful, playful, and energetic little boy with a lot to deal with. Among other things Toby has been diagnosed with severe global development delay, epilepsy, spasticity, osteoporosis, and cortical visual impairment. These conditions mean that Toby spends most of his time in a wheelchair, apart from an hour a day, when he can use his standing frame.

Because Toby is severely disabled my parents (Toby's grandparents) haven't been able to look after him and get involved in the way most grandparents can, so it meant so much to have them with us, they could have cuddles in bed with him in the morning and snuggle up to him watching telly in the afternoon, watch him splash about in the hot tub, and join in playing games. We made memories that will be with us forever.

Because of Toby's condition we never know what's round the corner and now he's facing puberty we have a new fear that the epilepsy may come back with a vengeance and could kill him. Until we get through puberty, we have no way of knowing how Toby will be in the future or how long he will live, we hope he will have the same quality of life he currently has but it could deteriorate so every second counts.

Thank you from the bottom of our hearts, I'm welling up just writing this, it's these little breaks that help us recharge and keep going. So much of our life is taken up with hospital appointments and therapies and medications and even though the break was just 3 nights it made such a difference to all our well beings.

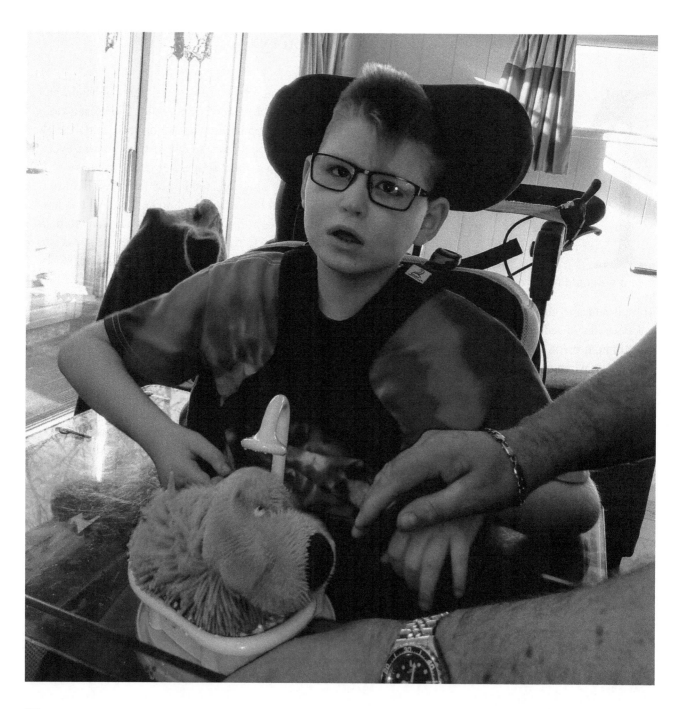

The Johnson' Family Story

Our son James is 9 years old and suffers badly from severe autism. The last family holiday we had with him was over three years ago. Due to his illness that holiday just did not work out. The holiday turned out to be anything but a holiday and was extremely hard work looking after James, as his autism was affected by the environment and the surroundings which meant he was very unwell for the whole time. Therefore, we have been very reluctant to go away on holiday since then as we do not want a repetition of the last holiday.

However, The Principle Trust Children's Charity offered us a free holiday at their lodge in the quiet surroundings of Ribblesdale Park in the Ribble Valley. After discussing and finding out more about the location, the surroundings, and the quieter nature of the lodge, despite being apprehensive about it, we decided we would accept the very generous offer and booked for a week away with James.

From the minute we arrived at the lodge, until the minute we left, we could not have been more pleased with the holiday and the terrific effect it had on James. It was just perfect.

Due to his condition he hardly ever sits still for any length of time, but he did on this holiday. He so enjoyed the walks in the beautiful, quiet countryside, and enjoyed looking for animals and was so excited when he saw rabbits, the peacocks roaming around the site, and some deer too. He wanted to go out walking every day, even the day it rained!

At no time did he try to run away which he does if he becomes stressed or agitated. He sat for long lengths of time reading books and watching tv.

His favourite time was sitting in the hot tub. Due to his illness, he rarely makes eye contact with us or people. But in the hot tub he would sit for ages looking at us, making lengthy eye contact, connecting, smiling at us, and listening to us telling stories. This time with James bought tears to our eyes.

This holiday was just fantastic in so many ways and taught us that there were things and times which James would and could enjoy and be with us without running away when he was stressed, enjoying so many simple things.

The whole holiday was a fantastic experience, and the memories will stay with us forever.

Thank you so much to the Charity for this opportunity which taught us so much about our son. A 'big thumbs up' from us all and especially James!

The Simpson Family Story

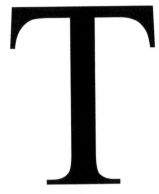The charity came to hear about this particular family from North Yorkshire County Council Children's Services. In an email to us they put forward the Simpson family for a free holiday, as they felt they were very much in need of a break away due to their difficult circumstances caring for their profoundly disabled son.

The parents went on to explain that it is very tiring (both physically and mentally) and stressful caring for their profoundly disabled son, it impacts the whole family. Their little boy cannot walk or communicate and needs 24/7 care. He is totally reliant on his mum and dad / those people caring for him. Unfortunately, due to this this means that it can take time away from them spending quality time with their daughter. They said they all really needed a rest and some quality time together. They spend a lot of time due to their son's needs in hospital and attending various appointments so a change in routine and a change of environment would be of huge benefit to them all.

This is exactly the kind of family that The Principle Trust Children's Charity looks to support. We were delighted to offer the Simpson family a free holiday break in one of our specially adapted disabled holiday homes. These holiday homes have wheel chair ramps, the doors have been widened so that wheel chair users can move around the home freely, the bathroom has been adapted into a wet room to make showering easier, and feature a profiling bed and hoist.

Upon the family's return from their holiday, we received a lovely thank you letter from the mum. She said "the holiday has definitely helped us a family unit, there were lots of activities on site that both children were able to access and enjoy. Our daughter was able to make friends with other children on holiday and join them in fun activities like the organised entertainment on offer and swimming. We could also split up (1 parent & 1 child) giving quality time to each child and access different entertainment on the holiday park site, knowing we were able to return easily to the facilities at the holiday home nearby if we needed to – which was particularly helpful for caring for our disabled son whilst we were away."

"We thoroughly enjoyed all of the holiday but the best part of our holiday was spending quality time together as a family and having such easy access to so many wonderful facilities which were close by to the holiday home."

"It was fabulous for us to have the opportunity to go on this holiday, and it was not too far us to travel to. Which is something we need to bear in mind whilst going anywhere. There was also lots to do in all weathers, which we were thankful for as the British Summertime is not something that can be relied upon. We had a truly wonderful time on holiday and would like to thank all at The Principle Trust Children's Charity from the bottom of our hearts. This holiday was so special to us, you do not know how much opportunity has meant to us all! It was fantastic to see both our children smiling and enjoying themselves once again, and doing what children should be doing and just having fun."

The outside seating area at the lodge at White Cross Bay, Windermere.

Tilly's Family Story

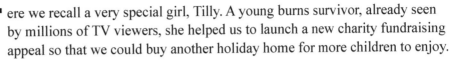

ere we recall a very special girl, Tilly. A young burns survivor, already seen by millions of TV viewers, she helped us to launch a new charity fundraising appeal so that we could buy another holiday home for more children to enjoy.

Brave eight-year-old Tilly has had more than 500 operations after only being given a 5% chance of survival. Tilly suffered fourth degree burns to 86 per cent of her body after falling into a scalding bath when she was just 15 months old. Her brother had accidentally turned on the hot tap and Tilly – who had been playing in the bathroom – fell in head-first.

Tilly, who has had her leg amputated after her family and medics agreed it was the best option to help alleviate the pain, first came to the attention of the Charity after she starred in the ITV show Love Your Garden with Yorkshires own Alan Titchmarsh and his team of garden designers earlier this year.

Her inspirational mum, Emma, said: "The Principle Trust Children's Charity have given us the chance to have a holiday together when without them this would not be possible. Tilly is really excited and will really enjoy the time out with the family during her on going treatment.

Principle Trust Children's Charity's Development Manager said "We wanted to do something special for Tilly and her family, especially after her amputation. Tilly is amazingly upbeat and positive, and we wanted her to be one of the children featured by the Charity to show how a holiday can help children and families.

Tilly went on to meet with her idols girl band - Little Mix, and amazingly went on to win the Child of Courage Award at The Pride of Britain Awards! Here is what one of the judges had to say about Tilly:

"Tilly's story is heart-breaking, but her positivity shines through. She is the most incredible example of the power of the human spirit. She has been through so much, yet she is still smiling and thinking of others."

Principle trust Children's Charity are absolutely delighted to let you all know that Tilly, the amazing little girl who is the face of our Charity has been told she has won the Child of Courage Award 2016.

Tilly was asked to go to London and was surprised by her absolute favourites, Little Mix, who broke the news that she had won the award which will be presented at the ITV Pride of Britain Awards on ITV November 1st. Thank you Little Mix, you have made this special little girls year !!!

Principle Trust
CHILDRENS CHARITY

'Mila's' Family Story

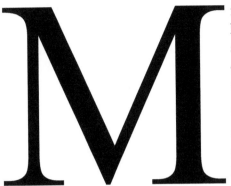ila has Spastic Quadriplegic Cerebral Palsy with severe dystonia. Mila has silent aspiration and is fed all nutrition via a gastrostomy. When she becomes ill (she is prone to chest infections) the infection can cause a dystonic storm. This can create respiratory distress due to the strength of the spasms in her neck.

We have been waiting for 2 years to be approved for adaptions in our house. We currently have nothing and as a result we have been assessed and told not to bathe her at home as we don't have the facilities. When well enough I take Mila to school and bathe her there. Or to the local pool where they have a "changing place" facility.

Mila favourite thing in the world is hydrotherapy as this has a relaxing effect on her spasms and relieves her body from all the contortions it is forced into on a daily basis. When Mila is well enough, she attends school and has access to a hydro pool once a week. Unfortunately, Mila cannot quite cope with the temperature of our local swimming pool.

My little girl and I have had the most amazing time at your cabin in Ribblesdale. Due to Mila's complex needs and ongoing unresolved medical issues we struggle to go too far from home as our local hospital knows her best and we are quite regular guests at their children's ward.

We spent time relaxing in the lovely cabin, enjoyed strolls to the cafe to enjoy their delicious food and open fire (great customer service here and made to feel really welcome). Splashed about in the hot tub, and cuddles on the sofas!

Our house is quite small, and we struggle to entertain guests around her equipment. Whilst at the cabin we had our friends come and visit us, we went for walks, ate at the café, and played in the hot tub. The open plan living room and kitchen meant that everyone could enjoy their time together happily and safely.

Mila doesn't sleep well due to pain and discomfort and we're often "up and about" at all hours. The layout of the cabin is perfect for this as we simply made a big bed out of both sofas and cuddled up together (me with a cup of tea of course!).

Garbutt Family Story

Wow! What a wonderful week we had at your log cabin. It may just be 15 minutes away from home but it's just what we needed.

I look after my grandson's full time; one is autistic and in heart failure and will shortly be listed for transplant. The little one has had a tracheotomy, pacemaker, is tube fed, and on a night is ventilated on a life support machine. Their Mummy has been diabetic since 8 years old and last week collapsed with clots in her lungs and heart.

I was exhausted and truly needed a few days to recharge. The boys have been here on and off but go home at night due to nurses coming in to care for my grandson and it enables my daughter to get sleep. You don't know what this break has meant to me and not just me but my children too. I've attached a few pictures of our stay which honestly has recharged my batteries.

Thank you to all at The Principle Trust for the kindest you have shown my family."

To Jess
+ all at the Principal
Twgg

We had a wonderful week
(could not stay the full week
as I was Fixed doing the
nights as at home
we have a nurse that comes in
· Thank you so much from
the bottom of heart
Hattie, Nicola + the boys

Snippets Of Stories From Families With Disabled Children, Or Children With Complex Health Conditions.

You don't know what this break
has meant to me. And not just
me but my children too."

#OurYorkshireChildren

The lodge is amazing, there was so much room for the kids to play. It was so comfortable and in a very quiet place so much that my little boy did not have to use his ear defenders at all on the park as it was peaceful and calming for him. The hot tub was great for his hypo- mobility and eased the pain in his legs, which helped him to sleep.

We explored the grounds doing lots of walks, which both children found very exciting especially when he saw the deer and peacocks. They all loved playing in the stream too. Both children have coordinated issues but tried so hard to ride their bikes as the park was very quiet had lots of space to practice.

We also enjoyed a lovely meal on our last night in the restaurant; the staff were very nice and placed us in a quiet spot in the restaurant. Overall, we had an amazing and relaxing time. A big thank you for letting us stay."

"It is very tiring both physically and mentally caring for our profoundly disabled son. It impacts the whole family. Our son can not walk or communicate and needs 24/7 care. He is totally reliant on us. Unfortunately, this can take time away from our young daughter."

#OurYorkshireChildren

"Our child has autism, developmental coordination disorder, cerebral visual impairment, hyper mobility, sensory processing disorder and has now been diagnosed with juvenile idiopathic arthritis. So being offered a free respite break in a home that caters to our child's needs almost seemed like a miracle."

#OurYorkshireChildren

The Principle Trust
Children's Charity

making memories that last

"From the moment we arrived, the kids were so excited to see the fabulous lodge and everything on offer around it."

#OurYorkshireChildren

In some cases, it will be the only holiday that some terminally ill children will have had or will have in their whole lives.

Honestly, what you are doing for families is incredible. This week has done more for my mental health than any counselling or drugs ever could. Just thank you. It was a really nice change. I came back feeling energised, fitter and not as down. Thank you so much.

We were contacted by a hospice to ask if a family with a very sick little boy could visit the lodge in Gisburn. Of course, we agreed, and everything was arranged for the little boy, his mum and dad, and his grandma and grandad to visit in late March 2020. Very regrettably, and so sad, that we were contacted to say the little boy had passed away. However, we were asked if the mum and dad, grandma and grandad could still go for the same time and use the time to remember and grieve for the little boy. How could we do anything but agree. The family were so grateful and sent us such a lovely message after their visit."

111

"In some cases it will be the only holiday that some terminally ill children will have had or will have in their whole lives."

#OurYorkshireChildren

The Principle Trust
Children's Charity

making memories that last

"Our autistic child doesn't often give us eye contact but when we were in the hot tub, we felt we were connecting and had lots of eye contact and smiles which brought a tear to our eyes."

#OurYorkshireChildren

"It was fabulous to have this
opportunity to go on holiday.
We had a truly wonderful time."

#OurYorkshireChildren

I would like to thank you from the bottom of our hearts we had a fantastic relaxing family time.

The lodge exceeded all our expectations, and we were able to drive the local places in The Lakes like the Beatrix Potter museum.

One of the highlights was watching baby bunnies been fed by their mummies at night.

Thank you so so much. x"

"Just thank you. It was a really nice change. I came back feeling energised, fitter and not as down. I know my grandson feels the same. Thank you so much."

#OurYorkshireChildren

"It was the last time we were able to spend time together as a family before our child passed away from a terminal illness."

#OurYorkshireChildren

Just wanted to say a huge thank you to everyone for this wonderful holiday. We really appreciated it and really needed a break. Our family had a fabulous time and we have made some good memories. Thank you for your kindness.

The lodge at Ribblesdale Park was superb. It had the space and adaptions that were really important for our disabled son. The location was beautiful, and we are very grateful to have able to take a trip we otherwise would not have been able to afford."

making memories that last

" In the case of very many of our children it is often the only holiday of their lifetime, which is why the opportunity to go on a Principle Trust holiday means so much to them."

What Some Of Our Social Partners Have To Say About Working Alongside The Principle Trust

Karl Podmore

Disabled Children's Service Manager

North Yorkshire County Council

arl Podmore has been instrumental to the charity, from how the charity was conceptualised in the beginning to its development over the years. Karl is a qualified social worker and has worked in children's social care for the Council since 1983.

"I've remained in touch with The Principle Trust throughout the last ten years and kept up to date with the successful expansion of both the charity and the number of holiday homes available to children throughout the whole of Yorkshire not just North Yorkshire. The referral process, allocation, and administration of bookings have all been refined over time, and the relationship between us and the charity has developed. As my role has changed, to managing the council's Disabled Children's Service the charity echoed this by having accessible facilities to enable disabled children and their families to take advantage of having a holiday by the lake of Windermere or in a lodge in the countryside in the picturesque Ribble Valley.

Wendy Barrett

Scheme Manager

Craven Home Start

 Having worked from home continuously throughout the lockdown, whilst both home-schooling three of my children and caring for my elderly, isolating parents; as a single Mum it has been a challenging time to juggle and manage everything.

The week's holiday I was gifted by the Principle Trust has provided us with invaluable quality time where I have been able to dedicate 100% of my attention to my children. We have participated in activities and created memories that will last a lifetime. Thank you!"

Dawn Hufton

Family Support

Hollybank

 As a child I was very lucky to enjoy family holidays each year and I'm in a very lucky
position that my boys can have the luxury of this too!"

Diane Watts

Police and Community Fundraiser

Embrace - Child Victims of Crime Charity

 I was told about Principal Trust children's charity by a Rotarian friend.

His club had just had a presentation on the charity from Mike Davies and my friend was of the opinion that's the charity I work for, which is Embrace child victims of crime, could potentially have a future working with the Principal Trust children's charity.

I rang their Skipton office and was invited to come across for a chat.

And I was told that we could send families who were referred to us for holidays in their luxury caravans and The log cabin they had at that time.

I could see this was a great opportunity for Embrace and asked what they wanted from us in return i.e. payment?

I was told that no payment was required. No payment! I said. No payment they said. All we want is feedback to help us with our fundraising.

I couldn't believe my ears at the generosity of this offer and I graciously accepted.

Since then several families with children who've suffered from the most horrendous crimes have had Wonderful And often life changing holidays in the caravans.

And I made sure they always gave feedback!

Here at Embrace we are very grateful to Principal Trust for their generosity and kindness and reciprocate by helping out wherever we can. Our families have holidays which are both therapeutic and healing thanks to Mike and his amazing charity and hard-working staff."

Jayne Trofa

Carer Support Worker

Making Space

It has been an absolute delight and privilege to have been able to be work in partnership with the wonderful Children's Principle Trust.

It has enabled us at Making Space to further help families we support who are caring for their adult relative with mental health difficulties the opportunity of a free family holiday which without The Trust they would not have been able to afford. The amazement and happiness these breaks have given families where in the working environment we are in, of reduced funding or no free services anymore, blew them and us away too at this organisation's generosity and ingenuity of its scheme.

We hope it continues in its success to enable many more families to have holidays together and create their happy memories too."

Rachel Yeadon

Area Prevention Manager for Harrogate & Knaresborough

Children and Families' Service: Prevention

I wanted to write to express thanks and gratitude on behalf of the Harrogate and Knaresborough Prevention Service team for enabling us to provide an opportunity for the vulnerable families we work with to access holidays.

The family feedback we receive is delightful, parents and carers tell us children have the opportunity to do things they would otherwise not get the chance to do and the time away has proved invaluable in reconnecting as a family and taking time out from the mundane day to day struggles, they are facing.

The charity is providing an invaluable service for those who most need it and I hope it continues to do so, benefitting as many children and young people as possible who otherwise would not experience a holiday."

Chris Keene

Thursby Trust at West End Community Centre

 Our group serves a very deprived community & our families don't have the disposable income needed to go on excursions, holidays or visits to cultural venues.

That's why we've always worked hard with partners like the Principle Trust to provide opportunities for holidays for our children & families.

The expression 'a holiday of a lifetime' is much used by the general population, but it's most often used to describe one outstanding holiday out of many experienced over a period of time.

In the case of very many of our children it is often the only holiday of their lifetime, which is why the opportunity to go on a Principle Trust holiday means so much to them.

I have adults who speak to me with such affection about the happy memories they have of the one time they went away on holiday with us & they remember all the details of the things they did.

The Principle Trust does an amazing job providing high quality opportunities for vulnerable children & families. So keep up the good work & we're really looking forward to returning to Blackpool later in the year!"

Anni Wilkinson

Programme Manager

Children's Services

It has been great opportunity for me meeting with you to understand more about your wonderful organisation and how it is funded etc.

I wanted to give you some insight into how the caravans have been used across our Children Services. The service you provide is so much more than just a holiday.

The holidays were offered across the whole of Children's services. I have direct links with three of those departments, residential services, fostering services and children with complex health needs.

This summer was particularly challenging for our residential services due to the warm weather. Young people were spending more time outside of the children's homes and there were various issues across the district with managing young people. Some of those young people fell into the looked after category.

Having the holidays booked in place meant that we were able to break the summer cycle and allow staff to re-engage with our young people in order to support them and address some of the issues encountered by the local community. In one of our residential homes, we also had the arrival of one young person that would have benefitted from more intensive support. The caravan allowed us a space to carry out closer therapeutic support for this young person by removing two of the other children in the home and allowing him to settle in while the others enjoyed an amazing time in Blackpool.

Within the fostering service, coming into care can be really overwhelming for some young people. Having a holiday with the Principle Trust allowed one family to have some neutral ground to 'get to know each other better'. The social workers also reported how fantastic this trip had been in allowing the foster parents to make some special memories with the children and young people in their care.

The introduction of the complex health cabin has been incredibly well received. These families have enjoyed the quieter setting of the holiday park. For one single parent family, having a break away for her and her daughter has been amazing as they have faced various difficult challenges over the past year.

Thank you so much for including us in this wonderful opportunity."

Lisa Finnett

Health Visitor

Harrogate District NHS

Harrogate and District
NHS Foundation Trust

Principle trust Holidays are an invaluable resource to families in need in the Craven area. As a Health Visitor for local families I have witnessed the real difference the holidays make to families.

Parental relationships are the most important influence on a baby/ child's development. The quality of this relationship is key to that child having successful outcomes in life. The Principle Trust holidays allow families who have been overwhelmed and struggling a chance to re-connect and focus on the child. This time away strengthens bonds and improves the parent-child relationship building more secure attachments which has far reaching benefits to the child after the holiday has ended and improves their overall development.

The holidays provided by The Principle Trust allow families, who often through no fault of their own, are going through adverse life experiences a chance to relax and switch off the stress flight/fight response in all family members which has numerous health benefits. Adverse childhood experiences such as domestic violence, parental separation, parental mental health issues, to name a few, have very harmful effects on children. Children growing up in families with such adversity are more likely to experience long term health issues, poor self-esteem, mental health issues and partake in risk taking behaviours. This is because the stress they experience physically alters the baby's/child's growing brains and affects their genetic predispositions. The holidays provide families caught in the hardships of life the opportunity to lift the burdens of life for a short time and become refreshed which in turn enables them to parent more positively. This sense of relaxation lasts beyond the week holiday and again improves life for the child long after the holiday ends particularly impacting positively on their brain development.

Another benefit of the holidays is that early childhood experiences stimulate the brain creating millions of connections. Hearing the sound of the waves, feeling the sand and being somewhere totally new give children who otherwise would not have these experiences a new view of the world. It stimulates their senses and helps lay the foundations for learning.

Most of all families' feedback that the opportunity to have a holiday gave them hope. Hope of a better future and hope more good opportunities will come their way. It restores faith that despite experiencing hard times the world is still good and things can get better.

It is often the most vulnerable children who benefit from these holidays and they deserve to have something good happen in life amidst the chaos and adversity they often have to endure and that is the biggest reason I think The Principle Trust is a fantastic charity. I would like to thank the Principle Trust on behalf of all my families that have benefited from a holiday for the important work they do to make life better for local children."

Charity Events and Fundraising

Martin Hendron starting the sponsored cycle ride from Lands End to John O'Groats.

**A**ny charity depends on fundraising, events, grants, and donations. We are no different.

We have undertaken several and varied events, and fundraising ideas during the 10 years of our existence which have not only been undertaken by charity staff, but also company staff, volunteers, friends of the charity, and family members.

Given we are now 10 years old and have added to the holiday homes to reach five homes, all totally owned by the Charity then we must be doing something right!

There are two areas of fundraising:

One is where a staff member is charged with identifying and applying to organisations for grants, and making applications for us to be chosen as a recipient of a grant etc… from the organisation whom has offered a sum of money to charities for worthy causes. In the majority of instances this money has been saved towards the holiday homes. This gives the donating organisation something tangible that their donation will be used for. We have raised in the region of £350,000+ to enable us to purchase 3 luxury caravans at Haven Holidays at Marton Mere in Blackpool, also to pay in full for two lodges, one at Ribblesdale Park in Ribble Valley, and one at White Cross Bay in the Lake District.

However, buying the homes is only the start of the venture!

The running costs for the holiday homes is a far greater than the cost of buying the units. We need to raise in the region of £10,000 - £11,000 per home per year to cover and afford the payments of running the homes.

We have to pay ground rent/site fees to the holiday park, all utilities i.e., water, gas, electricity, insurance, rates, call out fees for damages/problems, annual checking of utilities, security, cleaning of the homes, and laundry. Repairs and renewing items in every home. Updating, re modernising, replacements, and repairs. The more the homes are used the more the cleaning costs. In one home we have a hot tub maintained by the park particularly the water in the hot tub. The water pump has been replaced on the hot tub which cost 00's of ££! Of course, accidental damage happens and needs repairing/replacing.

Thus, we need to raise in the region of £55,000 per annum just to maintain and pay the bills for the homes! The more homes we have, the more the cost is of running them!

Our fundraising down the years has been various and fun.

Some of the events (and photographs included) are: (with apologies for any which I have omitted or forgotten!) Not in order of importance or ££ raised!

- The Annual Ball (held 8 times)
- Marathon runs (3 times)
- The 3 Peaks Challenge (undertaken 3 times)
- Dragon boat racing (twice)
- Skipton Point to Point Horse Racing
- Santa Fun Runs
- Skipton Xmas Markets
- Big Skipton, and Big Ilkley Quizzes
- Horse Race Evenings
- Silver Cross Tough Mudder
- Canal Boat Racing
- Mount Kilimanjaro Climb
- Afternoon Tea Events
- Digital Music Quiz
- Easter Egg Raffles
- Ilkley Carnival Duck Race
- John O'Groats to Lands End bike ride
- Road marathon
- Dalesway walk
- Spanish mountain climb
- Ebay selling of donated items
- Supermarket bag packing (in conjunction with local Scout groups)
- Rotary Club events and donations

To name but a few of the many events we have been involved in throughout the years.

To raise circa £55,000 per annum just to keep the homes running and provide circa 200 weeks holiday (during a normal year) for children takes a significant amount of fundraising and a great deal of time, effort, and planning.

A special word of thanks to the staff whom have been involved in the Charity since 2011, without their efforts we would not be where we are today, nor would so many underprivileged, disadvantaged, and disabled children and families, carers, been able to have enjoyed a free holiday.

Thank you sincerely.

Sponsored cycle from Lands End to John O'Groats.

Fraser fundraising for the duck race at Ilkley Carnival

Ilkley BNI volunteers collecting the ducks at the end of the race at Ilkley Carnival

Skipton Ford toy appeal

Lester Hurst, Mike Davies, and Andrew Procter

Santa fun run

Fundraising at Skipton Waterways Festival

The team at Silver Cross taking part in the Tough Mudder challenge, Skipton.

Silver Cross presenting the Charity with a cheque after completing the Tough Mudder challenge.

Race night

Yorkshire 3 Peaks fundraising walk

Tombola stall at Skipton Christmas Markets

The Big Skipton Quiz

Ilkley Christmas teepee event

Simon, Trustee and Matt fundraising by walking the Liverpool to Leeds canal.

Trek to the Lost City

Bake sale

Fundraising at Tesco Supermarket in Skipton

Ilkley Rotary Club presenting the charity with a cheque

Mike Davison, Louise Roberts, and Mike Davies MBE at The Big Quiz Night.

Buckingham Palace

Her Majesty The Queen

Mike Davies talking with Her Majesty The Queen after having received
The Queen's Award for Enterprise, International Trade in 2012.

In 2012, the year after establishing the children's charity I had the privilege of attending Buckingham Palace for an evening function along with other recipients of 'The Queens Award for Enterprise for International Trade'. This was a company award won by Principle Healthcare.

During the reception members of the Royal Family circulated and chatted with people present.

The Queen, The Duke of Edinburgh, Prince Edward, and The Duke of Kent mingled amongst the attendees.

I wanted to speak with Her Majesty, to tell her about my company but also the Children's Charity.

I was fortunate that Her Majesty came to speak to me, held out her hand to shake hands, albeit very lightly and asked me about my company. I told Her Majesty about the link between the company and the Charity and she was very interested, asking many questions about the Charity, the children, the facilities, the benefits. And I said "cheekily" that I would write to her once a year to inform her of the Charity's developments. She replied with a "yes please" and wished us well with our endeavours.

This had to be one of the most exciting discussions I had ever had in my life. The photograph of Her Majesty, and the "back of my head" shows Her Majesty smiling at something I had said. I cannot recall what that was.

However, every year I send a letter to Her Majesty, and every year we receive a response from one of her Ladies in Waiting. I always send the letter before the Annual Ball, and the reply always wishes everyone attending the Ball to have a most enjoyable evening, which I read out to the audience at the Ball. If Her Majesty says "enjoy the evening and she hopes it will be a success" whom am I to argue!

One year we had sent the letter but had no reply about four days before the Ball. Then we received a telephone call from Buckingham Palace from one of Her Majesty's Ladies in Waiting, profusely apologising that they had not replied to my letter. She asked if she could fax a response to us and put the original letter special delivery to us. Of course, that was all extremely nice to think of us and sure enough we received a Fax response, and the original landed in advance of the Ball. How kind to go to such lengths to reply to us!!

Some examples of the annual letters from Buckingham Palace are included in the book.

BUCKINGHAM PALACE

25th March, 2013

Dear Mr. Davies,

I have been asked to thank you, the Trustees and staff members of the Principle Trust for your kind letter to The Queen, sent on the occasion of your second Annual Charity Ball which is being held on 6th April at the Majestic Hotel in Harrogate.

Her Majesty was interested to learn that you are extending your work to assist the Women's Refuge of Thameside in Manchester. The Queen has asked me to convey her best wishes to all those attending the Ball for a memorable and enjoyable evening.

Yours sincerely,

Christopher Sandamas
The Chief Clerk to The Queen

Mike Davies, Esq.

162

31st January, 2014

Dear Mr Davies

The Queen wishes me to write and thank you for your letter and for the thoughtful sentiments which you expressed.

Her Majesty thought it kind of you to tell her of the ways in which the work of the Principle Trust is being extended to assist the Women's Refuge of Tameside in Manchester, the Outreach Programmes of Harrogate and York, and Lancashire Social Services.

The Queen was touched by your tribute to the tireless work of your Trustees and Staff, and Her Majesty was interested to hear that you will be holding your third Annual Charity Ball on 15th February.

Although unable to write to you personally, The Queen hopes that the Ball will be a most successful and enjoyable occasion, and Her Majesty sends her good wishes to you all for the coming year.

Yours sincerely,

Annabel Whitehead

Lady-in-Waiting

Michael Davies, Esq.

BUCKINGHAM PALACE

10th February, 2015.

Dear Mr. Davies,

The Queen has asked me to thank you, the Trustees and staff members of the Principle Trust for your kind letter, sent on the occasion of your fourth Annual Charity Ball which is being held on 14th February at the Coniston Hotel, North Yorkshire.

Her Majesty was interested to learn of the support your charity has provided for underprivileged children and of your successful fundraising achievements over the last year.

The Queen has asked me to convey her best wishes to all those attending the Ball for a most memorable and enjoyable evening.

Yours sincerely,

Christopher Sandamas
The Chief Clerk to The Queen

Mr. Mike Davies.

22nd March, 2016.

Dear Mr. Davies,

    I have been asked to thank you for you kind letter to The Queen, sent on behalf of The Principle Trust on the occasion of your Fifth Annual Charity Ball which is being held on 23rd April at Craiglands Hotel in Ilkley.

    Her Majesty was interested to learn of your plans to open a fourth holiday home and of the hard work and dedication of all involved in the charity to provide seaside breaks for underprivileged children.

    The Queen sends her warm, good wishes to all concerned for a most successful and enjoyable gathering.

Yours sincerely,

Christopher Sandamas
Chief Clerk to The Queen

Mike Davies, Esq.

165

BUCKINGHAM PALACE

8th June, 2017.

Dear Mr. Davies,

The Queen has asked me to thank you for your kind letter sent on behalf of The Principle Trust Children's Charity on the occasion of your Sixth Anniversary Charity Ball which is being held on 9th June at the Coniston Hotel in Skipton.

Her Majesty was pleased to be kept informed of the ongoing efforts of the Trustees, staff and supporters in raising funds for a holiday home in the Yorkshire Dales.

The Queen sends her best wishes to all those attending the Ball for a memorable and successful event.

Yours sincerely,

David Ryan

David Ryan
Director, Private Secretary's Office

Mike Davies Esq.

BUCKINGHAM PALACE

6th February, 2018.

Dear Mr. Davies,

The Queen has asked me to thank you for your kind letter of
17th January on behalf of the Principle Trust Children's Charity, on the
occasion of your Seventh Anniversary Charity Ball and Sixteen years
of Principle Healthcare which are being celebrated on 10th March at the
Coniston Hotel.

Her Majesty appreciated your thoughtfulness in writing as you
did and, in return, has asked me to send her warm good wishes to all
those who will be present for a most successful and enjoyable event.

Yours sincerely,

David Ryan

David Ryan
Director, Private Secretary's Office

Mr. Mike Davies, MBE.

BUCKINGHAM PALACE

6th March 2019

Dear Mr Davies,

The Queen wishes me to write and thank you for your letter.

Her Majesty thought it kind of you to tell her of the many ways in which the Principle Trust Children's Charity has helped underprivileged and disabled children throughout Yorkshire, by providing holidays for them and their families.

The Queen was touched by your tribute to the tireless work of your Trustees, staff and supporters, and Her Majesty was interested to hear that you will be holding your Annual Charity Ball on 6th April.

Although unable to write to you personally, The Queen hopes that the Ball will be a most successful and enjoyable occasion, and Her Majesty sends her good wishes to you all for the coming year.

Yours sincerely,

Richenda Elton

Lady-in-Waiting

Mr M Davies MBE

Charity Events At The Coniston Hotel

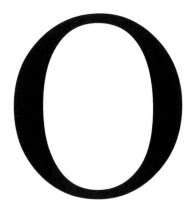One of the highlights of each year since we started the Charity in 2011 is The Annual Charity Ball.

The Charity was launched at The Coniston Hotel, at Coniston Cold in North Yorkshire in January 2011 and we have held the Ball at The Coniston almost every year, except for two years when they did not have availability. In those two years we held the Ball elsewhere but went back to The Coniston!

We have held 8 Annual Balls, of which six have been at The Coniston. We know we are in safe, good quality hands when we are at The Coniston. The 9th ball should have happened during 2020, on July 4th with a Stars and Stripes Theme, but the pandemic meant everything was cancelled. We aim to have our 10th Anniversary Ball at The Coniston.

The Bannister family whom own the hotel are great friends of the Charity and help us in many ways. Michael Bannister is the owner, and his son Nick runs the hotel aided by Louise Bolton the General Manager.

Not only is it a great venue set in beautiful surroundings, but the hotel, rooms, facilities, food, staff, and service are excellent.

In addition to The Annual Ball, the Bannisters have helped us with being a selected Charity in the Skipton Point to Point horse racing, which is a great day out set-in lovely surroundings.

They also allow the Dragon Boat Racing on the estate lake which our charity get involved in. A really good day out for all the family (made all the better by the good weather!).

The staff also partake in other events such as the Three Peaks Walk, covering 3 of the highest peaks in North Yorkshire across a 24 mile walk, and obtain sponsorship for the charity.

The Canal Rowing Challenge in Skipton, hoping that the boat does not capsize!

In return we endeavour to hold the Annual Ball at the hotel every year! It is a lovely place to be, and The Bannisters are a really supportive family, and good friends. Long may that be the case!

Nick Bannister presenting Mike Davies MBE with a cheque for the Charity

Annual Ball at The Coniston Hotel

Andrew Davies, Trustee and supporters at the Valentine's Ball, Coniston Hotel. Sponsored by JCT600.

Mike Davies MBE, Clare Campbell, Trustee with supporters at Annual Charity Ball at The Coniston Hotel.

Friday 9th June 2017

Thank you for joining us
in celebrating...

The Principle Trust
Children's Charity
6th Anniversary
and
Principle Healthcare
15th Anniversary
Annual Ball

The Coniston Hotel

Philip Davies and Andrew Davies, Trustee at the Annual Charity Ball at the Coniston Hotel.

Clare Campbell, Trustee at the Annual Ball held at The Coniston Hotel.

'Captain' Andrew Davies, Trustee at the Dragon Boat race at The Coniston Hotel.

Simon Thomas, Trustee with 'HMS BNI Ilkley' at the Dragon Boat Race at The Coniston Hotel.

Whole supporters team at the Dragon Boat Race at The Coniston Hotel

Skipton Races Point to Point

BNI Ilkley's Support With Fundraising and Events

I am a great believer in networking with people and companies and have several positive reactions and collaborations during my career due to networking. Even if meeting someone for the first time is friendly but not fruitful for mutual business, you just never know what may transpire in the future.

I received an invitation in 2019 from someone I had never met, but knew of, asking me if as a Founder and Trustee of a Charity I would like to attend a meeting as his guest, with BNI. There is a branch of BNI in Ilkley, the town where I live, and I readily agreed. He explained that this group do not have a Charity Membership within their group and would like to have one.

BNI stands for Business Network International, and a surprise to me was that there are in excess of 285,000 members worldwide. BNI is the world's largest Networking and Business Referral Organisation.

The BNI membership mainly consists of small to medium size businesses where members/owners meet, network together, and gain referrals, for business development. They meet weekly to discuss their business and work together on referrals.

It is an exclusive membership with only one type of business allowed to be members, no duplication.

I enjoyed the meeting and found much interest about the Charity amongst the members, and after two visits to the meeting decided that we should join the organisation. I believed that the Charity would benefit from membership, with a number of the companies saying they would like to "adopt and support the charity". Clearly many people wanted to help underprivileged, disadvantaged, and disabled children! I also believed that the commercial businesses I owned could enjoy a mutual interest in being involved in BNI. Thus, my son whom is the MD of the commercial businesses and a Trustee of the Charity became the person whom joined BNI.

Since then, there have been several two way, mutually advantageous networking with tangible benefits to BNI and to the commercial business.

Likewise, the Charity have benefitted enormously from membership with almost all of the members becoming involved personally and with their companies in fundraising for the Charity.

A number of the events which BNI Ilkley have been involved in are:

Ilkley Carnival Duck Race, members attempting to retrieve 2000 plastic ducks from the River at the end of the race! Cold and wet, but successful!

The BNI dragon boat crew coming runners up in The Coniston Hotel Dragon Boat Race!

3 Peaks challenge.

Dalesway walk.

Spanish mountain climb.

Cleaning and maintaining the holiday homes.

TeePees and food and drink for children, and supporters of charity at Christmas. It was a great moment to meet in person some of the children and families we have helped!

Banyan quiz night.

Helping and assisting charity printing, apparel, leaflets, insurance, websites, carpets, and flooring etc…

Providing items for Christmas gifts for children.

Delivery of items during pandemic.

Providing a video for use by the Charity.

The offer of publishing this book about the first 10 years of the Charity came through our membership of BNI Ilkley. What a terrific gesture!

These are but a few of the BNI Ilkley fundraising and helpful areas where the Charity has benefitted. The BNI target of £11,000 in year one was well beaten, which went a long way to pay the operational costs for two holiday homes for almost a year.

There is no doubt that networking works!

Thank you BNI and especially the membership of Ilkley. Long may our networking association last!

Martyn, BNI Enterprise (Ilkley) and his climbing partner completed a sponsored climb of the Penon in Calpe, Spain.

Martyn, BNI Enterprise and his climbing partner at the summit of Penon in Calpe, Spain.

BNI Enterprise taking part in the Dragon Boat Race fundraiser at The Coniston Hotel.

Dominic Hernon, BNI Enterprise and Rhys Jones from UK Global who successfully completed a 26-mile charity walk from Leeds to Skipton.

The Pandemic Year
2020 (and 2021)

veryone involved in the Charity was looking forward to 2020 being the biggest year for children and families enjoying a free holiday.

Plans had been set for a record number of exciting events.

Haven Holiday Park at Blackpool was due to open for the start of the holiday season in mid-March. The caravans looked fantastic as we had completely refurbished them with new upholstery, new carpets, new bedding, new curtains, new equipment, and decorated many rooms.

Ribblesdale Park with our disabled lodge had been updated with many improvements both inside and outside.

Our new lodge purchased finally in November 2019, at White Cross Bay on the banks of Lake Windermere was due to be opened by the ex-England, Barbarians, British Lions Rugby International Peter Squires, on 12th February 2020. We had not made any bookings for this lodge as we still needed to obtain a disabled bed and an electric hoist. Likewise, we wanted to check all was complete and working before providing it to disabled children.

However, we were able to think about planning 99 weeks at Blackpool, 52 weeks at Ribblesdale Park and 38 weeks at Windermere. That was 189 weeks. A record for the Charity!

With 3 homes for underprivileged and disadvantaged children.

With 2 homes for disabled children.

Plenty of bookings had been placed with the caravans having about 70% occupancy, with Ribblesdale Park at 60% before the year started. We had lots of excited children looking forward to a free holiday.

Although some holidays went ahead at Ribblesdale Park, and three holidays went ahead after the opening of the new lodge at White Cross Bay, the "Pandemic Struck" and all holiday homes, and as a result children's holidays went into lockdown. No holiday parks open meant no holidays.

No fundraising events could take place.

Telephones were hot with calls postponing the holidays, asking "when the holiday parks would re-open", "can the holidays be carried over until later date?" All sorts of questions from mums and dads, foster parents, carers, social workers, and teachers, etc... Many questions we could not answer. We had to say no to dates later in the year due to the weeks already being booked. Plus, we had no idea what or when the Pandemic would abate and when we could offer dates from.

A really concerning time.

Then the events began to cancel. All internal events due to be held inside i.e., quizzes, The Annual Ball due to be held on 4ᵗʰ July. Then external events were cancelled like The Ilkley Carnival, Skipton Point to Point horse racing, and the London Marathon (which Andrew a Trustee had a place for!).

Our income was decimated, but our outgoings were also reduced due to significantly reduced costs of empty holiday homes.

We did plan and undertake some external socially distanced activity:

Simon Thomas a Trustee walked a marathon along the road he lives on, completing his task in one day! He also walked from Leeds to Skipton along the Leeds to Liverpool canal.

Andrew Davies a Trustee and friends, and others many from BNI walked The Dales Way walk from Ilkley to Windermere. 80+ miles across four days.

Phil Davies and others joined together to walk (or climb) the Yorkshire Three Peaks. Covering some 20+ miles in one day!

A number of other external events in the fresh air, maintaining social distancing raised some much needed funds for the Charity, ensuring we were able to retain the Sustainability Plan we have in place for the Charity.

Then the holiday parks could open, in a limited way.

We had cancelled and postponed the majority of pre-booked holidays, and despite contacting the families again there was, understandably some reticence in going to the parks, particularly as they were only "part open".

Thus, the Trustees decided to see whether the Key Workers, working at the frontline of the Pandemic in many, many areas would like to opportunity of a free holiday with their children.

We concluded that the aims of the Charity would still be applicable and that children of Key Workers could be classed as "disadvantaged "as many had not seen their parents for some weeks, many were not in contact with their children, and many parents at the front line deserved a break.

We decided that the key issue here was the family bonding again, and to help with the mental wellbeing of the whole family.

194

So, we offered up the holiday homes to Key Workers.

We were I am delighted to say, "overwhelmed with the responses".

We booked holidays for NHS nurses, doctors, porters, paramedics, care home workers, carers for the elderly, some teachers, some supermarket workers, the list of people were endless. Some of their stories brought tears to our eyes. Especially the consultant from a hospital whom had not been home for 6 weeks, not seen his children or wife, and slept at the hospital.

The responses we received from the Key Workers whom enjoyed a holiday were incredible. It fully justified our decision to help them and offer them free holidays.

Then lockdown came again, and everything closed once again. Back to square one. No parks or homes open, no family holidays, and no events.

The Charity remained focussed on applying for grants, sending applications and bids for relevant help and finance from many organisations whom were offering financial help and support. Every other charity was doing the same.

The Trustees and Staff of the Charity must be commended for their extreme hard work, dedication to the cause, retaining a positive outlook, helping each other with teamwork and planning for 2021 which is to be our 10th year anniversary!

Christmas Gift Appeal for Airedale Hospital

Kathryn who took part in our Christmas Gift Appeal for Airedale Hospital.

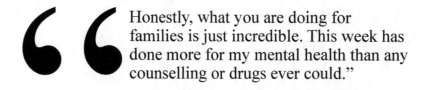

Honestly, what you are doing for families is just incredible. This week has done more for my mental health than any counselling or drugs ever could."

Key Workers Family Stories

The Desborough Family Story

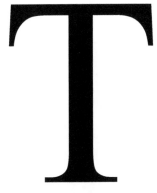he whole holiday has been full of beautiful memories. From puddle walks on a rainy day and seeing my little girl (21 months old) and her granddad (who has had a stroke) laughing hysterically as they play together, to spending the full day at the beach building sandcastles, paddling in the sea, and waving at horses. It has just been wonderful.

just want to say how incredibly grateful I am. I am a secondary English teacher and since the day my school closed I have spent every day including most evenings and every weekend on online classrooms, zoom calls or actually physically in school working with the children of other key workers and frontline staff. I have juggled this around having my 21 month old at home full time. I have had to work around her naps and needs meaning some days I have been working until 10.30pm. I worked every school holiday and was even physically in school on Easter Monday. All this while my profession was ripped apart at every opportunity in the national and local media. To be honest, it has been pretty soul destroying and I cannot deny that I have shed many tears. My dad is registered disabled following a stroke and my mum is his full time carer. It has been so hard not to see them and try and support them. This holiday meant I could completely switch off. The slightly patchy Wi-Fi meant I was not chained to my phone. I just enjoyed being with the people I love the most. After all the stress, worry and fear caused by COVID, this felt almost like normality and meant we could make memories we will treasure forever. Thank you so much.

Honestly, what you are doing for families is just incredible. This week has done more for my mental health than any counselling or drugs ever could. We have agreed as a family we will be sending a donation your way so you can continue to help other families. Hoping to get involved with some fundraising in the next year for you too!"

Moore Family Story

I just wanted to thank you all personally at The Principle Trust Children's Charity.

Our key worker holiday in Windermere has been just fantastic!

To give you an insight as to how the pandemic has been for us as a family… last year I gave up child minding after 11 years, our own children had to be put first and our eldest had been diagnosed autism. I became a support worker with The National Autistic Society. With the pandemic, this role has been incredibly challenging due to routines being disrupted causing behavioural issues that just cannot be helped for the adults I supported. I have had many 'wobbles' mentally wondering if I'm doing the 'right thing' but I work with a fabulous team and they have supported me no end. I have elderly relatives that I also support… basically everything had come all at once from all directions. This break has been a godsend!

"As a family we have spent time together (completely social distancing the whole world) but we are relaxed, we are stronger, we are happy, the lodge is gorgeous, and the site is lovely.

"You have made such a difference and we are so grateful to you all.

"What a wonderful charity.

"All our thanks and best wishes."

Khan Family Story

The whole break was fantastic from start to finish.

"It was lovely to have time together for the first time in months that wasn't the same four walls as home where the children have been stuck for so long. We have never all been to the beach altogether before and seeing the children play, build sandcastles have a donkey rides was fantastic this was my daughters favourite memory. My other daughters favourite memory was the bungee trampoline activity on the Haven site and my son rode his 1st proper rollercoaster at the Pleasure Beach theme park.

"My younger daughter also spotted a little crocheted doll in the drawer with the jigsaws she named it Dobby the caravan elf. As it looked like Dobby from Harry Potter! She loved talking to it and we put it on one of the shelves so it could look after us whilst we were in the caravan."

Snippets From Key Worker Family Stories

Both our sons loved the swimming every day. The fun, laughter, and togetherness definitely helped us as friends and family. Our 3-year-old learnt to float with an inflatable vest, previously they would not let go of us! The confidence in the water was a very special time. We looked forward to the swimming every day. We visited the zoo, beach, and even had picnics. We had a wonderful relaxing time.

Thank you so much The Principle Trust for giving us the chance to spend some time together this summer after a really tough year. My partner works in a supermarket and has been working of hour god sends, whilst I've been on furlough and looking after the children full time".

"Honestly what you are doing for families is incredible. This week has done more for my mental health than any counselling or drugs ever could."

#OurYorkshireChildren

"It was a great adventure and we had the best day of our lives. And now they keep looking at all of the photos we took and laughing."

#OurYorkshireChildren

"I needed this holiday because I needed to be me again for a short while and just be able to put me first for once."

#OurYorkshireChildren

This was the very first time our little one 16 months old experienced the seaside. She loved the beach, sand, pier-sides, and all the walks we got out on! Thanks again for selecting us, a holiday is not something we can afford every year, and especially this year due to the COVID-19 pandemic and subsequent lockdown. I'm a nurse at a local doctors surgery, and my husband has been on and off furlough for months. This is the first time in such a long time that we have spent some real time together."

"After all the stress, worry and fear caused by Covid this felt almost like normality and meant we could make memories we will treasure forever."

#OurYorkshireChildren

"It was the best ever thing you have done for us and I can't thank you all enough. Thank you for making us stronger as a family."

#OurYorkshireChildren

"The sense of relaxation lasts beyond the week holiday and improves life for the child long after the holiday ends, particularly impacting positively on their brain development."

#OurYorkshireChildren

The best bit was definitely winning a huge chocolate bar in the amusements! Spending time on the beach building sandcastles, flying my kite, and riding donkeys was also very good." Thomas aged 5, whose mum is a single parent, and front-line worker."

"I've had many wobbles mentally recently…this break has been a godsend. As a family, we have spent time together. We are relaxed, we are stronger, and we are happier. You have made such a difference and we are so grateful to you all."

#OurYorkshireChildren

"We are very grateful to have been able to take a trip that we otherwise would not have been able to afford."

#OurYorkshireChildren

"From the moment we arrived, the kids were so excited to see the fabulous lodge and everything on offer around it."

#OurYorkshireChildren

 Just being able to spend the time together as a family without all the distractions of life going on at the moment was a huge benefit to us all.

Due to the ongoing Covid-19 pandemic our children were extremely happy to spent some time away from their home and relax and enjoy alot of open spaces.

The close encounters with the deers and peacocks was a nice addition and exploring new areas."

making memories
that last

2021 - The Charity
10th Year Anniversary

Although the Charity was incorporated on 15th November 2010, we held the Charity's "Launch Ball" in January 2011 which officially put the Charity into existence, and the 140 people attending the Ball knew nothing about the Charity before the Ball but knew all about it afterwards!

As we headed towards our 10th year anniversary in January 2021, we knew that we would be heading into "unknown territory" with the COVID-19 pandemic, with uncertainty surrounding everything we had been planning for our 10th year. The closer we got to January, the more cancellations and postponements for activity happened.

The Trustees and Staff of the Charity had agreed that a real landmark for our 10th year would be to raise sufficient money to buy our 6th holiday home. It would be for disabled children and likely at Lake Windermere again. This remains our aim, however difficult it may be! This would then mean that we would have three holiday homes in Blackpool allowing circa 100 weeks per annum for holidays. Also, three disabled holiday homes, two at Lake Windermere, and one in Ribble Valley to allow 148 weeks. If, and it is a big "if" we are able to raise sufficient money for another holiday home it will mean that we will then have the space, and weeks, to offer circa 250 families a free holiday per year!

Never in our dreams did we think we would be able to reach this when we set out in 2011! Now we must raise the funds for the additional home!

We were able to notify all partners, friends, and supporters that 2021 was to be our 10th anniversary but had to postpone all plans until further notice. Our 10th year logo with "making memories that last" appeared, and a strategic rethink of activity took place.

All collective events were postponed, The Annual Ball was postponed until October, the local town events, the fun nights, the quizzes, the markets, the supporter events from Rotary and Round Table to name but a few were gone! Along with the much-needed funds normally raised!

We did plan to operate some events which could be socially distanced, outdoor events, which fingers crossed we can still go ahead with. A repeat of the Yorkshire 3 Peaks walk, which raised several thousand of £s in 2020.

Simon Thomas a Trustee and big fundraiser has a marathon walk around Ilkley planned, likewise a really big event being "The Olympic Cycle Home" ffrom London to Ilkley, with support from former Olympian Dudley Hayton.

We have also been busy developing the Charity Patron Scheme where businesses join as a Patron of the charity and subscribe monthly to us, in return for advertising their company, social media activity, and the companies using the Charity as their CSR Partner. It really is amazing to hear about the people whom view companies positively being involved with a children's charity. The companies and people whom have very generously become Patrons of the Charity are:

Sevensun
Rich Hayden

sevensun

Absolute Resin Surfaces
Lee Bailey

J.L. Bailey Insurance Brokers
James Bailey

Sovereign Wealth
Diane Watson

Greenholme Carpets and Flooring
Simon Thomas

Candid HR
Emma Harvey

Rinew Legal
Richard Newstead

TaxAssist Accountants
Julia Forrester

Secret Drawer
Richard Mason

Print Crew
Simon Raybould

Westrow Hair and Westrow Academy
Mark Westerman

UK Global Insurance Brokers Leeds
Dominic Hernon

Mobili Office
David Cock

The Mailman
Louis Sandford

Hunters Estate Agents and Letting Agents Ilkley and Otley
Lester Hurst

Hunters Estate Agents and Letting Agents Skipton
Andrew Procter

Sutcliffe Construction LTD
James Sutcliffe

With grateful thanks to all the Patrons for their support during very difficult times. We look forward to further assisting your businesses once lockdown allows.

We are developing an Individual Patrons Scheme where individual people can contribute monthly to the Charity. Any amount donated is really helpful, remembering that every £1 raised "goes towards the children's holidays".

It is with great pride and sincere thanks to the trustees, staff, patrons, supporters, and friends that we have been able to "stay afloat" during undoubtedly the worst period of time in most people's existence. We all sincerely hope that 2021 does "open up" and the COVID-19 pandemic gets controlled to enable countries everywhere to get back to a "new normal" and the Charity can begin to help the underprivileged, disadvantaged, and disabled children and families to enjoy a free holiday.

The Future – The Next 10 Years

Holiday home at Parkdean White Cross Bay Holiday Park, Windermere.

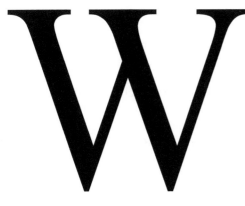

When we started up in January 2011, we never set targets for homes, children's holidays, or disabled holiday homes.

We now have five holiday homes, and have provided circa 3,600 children and parents, carers, foster parents etc… a free holiday in our 10-year existence so far.

What will the next 10 years bring?

Once again, we set no absolute targets on holiday homes, other than we will likely have to replace the 3 holiday caravans in Blackpool during the next decade which will cost us circa £135k to £150k in total. That will not provide any more holidays but will update 3 ageing caravans to new ones.

As stated, we are hoping to achieve another disabled home during our 10th year, which will mean six homes and 250 holidays per annum to fill.

If we are able to achieve another home in Blackpool, and another at Lake Windermere that would mean eight homes providing circa 350 free holidays for children per annum, that would be fantastic.

We have spoken about considering whether and if we could somehow obtain a unit or converted home at Lake Windermere to use for daily help, teaching, learning, and/or games for disabled children. That would be a real benefit to children and families from maybe four homes at Lake Windermere benefitting from some form of learning, help, and assistance. Only a thought so far, but something that could really add some much-needed help and value to families and children.

We also want to be able to gain much greater awareness of the Charity throughout Yorkshire. We have grown from a North Yorkshire Charity to one which has as much activity in West Yorkshire now. What about South and East Yorkshire? We are developing more holiday homes, thus more holidays, and we want to ensure that we are offering these to more needy children.

We aim to become more involved in communities and spread the word about our work and get lots of other people helping us to provide free holidays.

The Corporate Patrons Scheme is incredibly important to us, and we have a desire to get many more companies involved.

The Individual Patrons Scheme will be developed. To ask people to contribute £3 a month or more we believe will further enable us to provide the help and assistance we give to needy children.

We want to find an Ambassador for the Charity. Ideally someone from Yorkshire, maybe living here, or born here, and prepared to help us occasionally in our quest to help children.

So, here is to the next 10 years, with as much help from supporters as the last 10! As much fun and motivation that the past 10 years have provided for the people involved in the Charity.

I sincerely hope we can look back in 10 years' time with as much satisfaction as we are now!

Thank you to every single person whom has helped us during the past 10 years.

Acknowledgements

I am very, very sad to announce that a great personal friend for many years and a real supporter of the Charity, Mike Davison sadly passed away in August 2020.

Brenda and I have known Mike and his wife Adrienne for forty years, having lived very close to them in Preston, and our sons being much the same age and going to the same schools. We all became very good friends, socialising, and holidaying with them.

A keen golfer and a dab hand at Texas hold 'em (particularly on the tables in Las Vegas!) always enjoyed a good "craic" with a Guinness and Veda bread?!

Being a thespian Mike liked both appearing in, and directing plays for The Club Players at Broughton, particularly "comedies" where he was absolutely at home playing the humorous parts. Mike was Club President of Broughton and District Club in 2012 - 2013.

He spent his full career working for Gallahers, then having retired helped us in a number of areas in Principle Healthcare.

Mike and Adrienne were great supporters of the Charity. Mike ran many quizzes, race evenings (wearing the relevant regalia of course) and was Quizmaster at The Big Skipton Quiz.

Mike stepped in at the last minute when we were let down by Charles Hanson as Auctioneer at The Ball, and he excelled and did a terrific job in shaming people to part with their money!

Adrienne has kindly given her permission for this to be included in the book.

A smashing guy, a lovely wife, and family lost to us far too soon.

Rest in Peace Mike.

Mike Davison as our auctioneer at a charity event

Original Charity Trustees

Fiona Lazenby, Nicky Midgley and Clare Campbell with Founder and Chairman Mike Davies MBE.

Ann Harding Trustee at The Annual Charity Ball

Simon Thomas Trustee taking part in The Dales Way fundraising challenge

Special Thanks

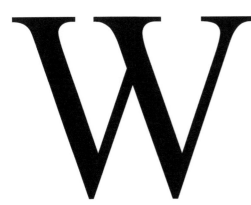ithin the following I have tried to detail and recall all those who have helped, supported, and assisted with the charity developments since inception in 2011.

To those I have forgotten, or inadvertently omitted, please accept my sincere apologies.

We could not have done it without you!

- My wife, Brenda – who stood by me, listened, and helped whilst I was trying to work out what to do to help less fortunate children.

- Phil, Andrew, Sarah and Ruth and our six wonderful Grandsons for being our inspiration and for bringing so much joy.

- Her Majesty The Queen Elizabeth II – whom had replies sent to my letter to her every year thanking us for the Charity work and wishing everyone a great time at The Charity Ball!

- HRH The Duke of Cambridge – for all his interest shown at my investiture with MBE and asking me to ensure everyone involved "keeps up the amazing work we do"!

- The original Principle Team – too many to name, but to a person you all gave the thumbs up to helping the cause.

- The first Trustees – to Clare, Nicky, and Fiona you were instrumental in helping set up the charity and get it working.

- Karl Podmore – from NYCC, who gave focus, ideas, and direction when we needed it most.

- Principle, Innopharma, Health Innovations, and Vitrition Management – for contributing finance monthly to the Charity to pay for the staff wages.

- All Charity Staff since 2011 – thank you for your help and contribution during your time with the charity.

- Rotary Clubs in Yorkshire – too many to name, thank you for your support and for the work you do in the community.

- Round Table and Inner Wheel – thank you for your help.

- Oddfellows Society – for adopting us and raising funds.

- Mike and Adrienne Davison – great supporters from day one and excellent function managers.

- John "Shoey" Shoesmith – Mr DIY in the holiday homes.

- Dave Robinson – for leading the Yorkshire 3 Peaks Challenge each year.

- Johnny B, Boyley, Phil H, and Andrew – for travelling from each part of the UK and giving of their time to walk the Dalesway.

- Diane from Embrace - for all you do for Embrace and our Charity.

- Paul and Julie Cooper for the 'Annual Easter Egg Extravaganza' which has raised significant amounts for the charity.

- The Coniston Hotel – Michael, Nick, and Louise for your help and generosity in so many ways.

- The Wooden Spoon Charity – for help at White Cross Bay lodge.

- Gaie Scouller – for your help at Ribblesdale Park lodge.

- BNI Ilkley – all team members for being such great sports and supporters.

- Neil and Nathalie Harrison – for your gaming chips and donations.

- Hunters Estate Agents- to Lester and Andrew for help, awareness, and contributions.

- All current patrons – your support is invaluable.

- David Rasche for continued support.

- Jean and John Coutts-Wiggins for your support throughout the years.

- Each and every charitable trust for providing us with much needed grants and donations.

- Simon Thomas – inspired choice for a Trustee, and what a supporter and fundraiser.

- Ann Harding - inspired choice for a Trustee, for help at Settle Victoria Hall and sharing her experience and skills in Charity work.

- Olivia Thomas and Kerry Magson – for their help with this book!

- Rich Hayden and Rick Armstrong - for providing us with the opportunity of publishing this book.

Making memories that last

The story of the first 10 years

Lightning Source UK Ltd.
Milton Keynes UK
UKHW051108061021
391733UK00005B/67